THE
ISLAMIC
TRADITION

MAJOR TRADITIONS OF WORLD CIVILIZATION
UNDER THE EDITORSHIP OF HAYDEN V. WHITE

THE
ISLAMIC
TRADITION

JOHN B. CHRISTOPHER

Professor of History
University of Rochester

HARPER & ROW, PUBLISHERS

NEW YORK, EVANSTON, SAN FRANCISCO, AND LONDON

Standard Book Number: 06-041283-6
Library of Congress Catalog Card Number: 72-77485

CONTENTS

Chronology   viii
Maps   xiv
Author's Note on the Spelling of Arabic Words   xvi
Editor's Introduction   xvii

Introduction: Two Images of Islam   1

The Arabian Setting   5

MECCA AND MEDINA   6
ARABS AND SEMITES   7
LANGUAGE AND POETRY   8
THE SHIFTING BALANCE OF POWER   10
THE ASCENDANCY OF MECCA   13
PRE-ISLAMIC RELIGION   14

The Prophet   16

THE CALL TO RECITE   18
PREACHING AND PERSECUTION IN MECCA   20
THE DECADE AT MEDINA   22

The Teachings of Islam   27

HADITHS   31
THE LAST JUDGMENT   34
MAN AND GOD   36

The Pillars of the Faith   39

CONFESSION OF FAITH   39
PRAYERS   40
ALMS   43
RAMADAN   44
THE HAJJ   46

The Law and the State   52

THE SHARIA   52
THE ULEMA   53
THE FOUR PATHWAYS   55
HUMAN CONDUCT AND HUMAN RIGHTS   56
THE CALIPHATE   59
A CENTURY OF EXPANSION   60
THE UMAYYADS, A.D. 661–750   63
THE ABBASIDS A.D. 750–1258   65
THE END OF THE CALIPHATE   68

Orthodoxy and Heterodoxy   70

SUNNIS AND DISSIDENTS   70
THE KHARIJITES   71
SHIISM   72
TWELVERS AND ZAIDIS   76
ISMAILIS AND ASSASSINS   77
ALAWIS AND DRUZES   80
BABIS AND BAHAI   83

Sufism   86

SUFISM DEFINED   86
THE PILGRIM'S WAY   89
DERVISH, SHEIK, AND BROTHERHOOD   91
THE URBAN ORDERS   93
THE RUSTIC ORDERS   94
LIABILITIES AND ASSETS   96
AL-GHAZALI   98

Philosophy   102

THE GREEK LEGACY   103
DETERMINISM AND FREE WILL   105
THE MUTAZILITES   105
THE PHILOSOPHERS: AR-RAZI   108
AL-FARABI   110

AVICENNA   112
AVERROES   115
IBN-KHALDUN   116

Science   119

MEDICINE   120
MATHEMATICS AND THE PHYSICAL SCIENCES 123
ASTROLOGY AND ALCHEMY   126
MUSIC   129

The Arts and Literature   132

THREE EARLY MONUMENTS   133
THE ISLAMIC STYLE   135
MOSQUES AND THEIR DECORATION   137
REGIONAL AND DYNASTIC VARIATIONS   140
SELJUKS, SAFAVIDS, AND OTTOMANS   142
PROSE LITERATURE   146
POETRY   149

The Modern Challenge   154

THE MUSLIM PEOPLES TODAY   154
NATIONALISM AND COMMUNISM   156
BLACK AFRICA   157
THE INNER CRISIS AND THE WAHABI
   RESPONSE   158
THE MUSLIM BROTHERHOOD   160
PAN-ISLAM AND ISLAMIC MODERNISM   162
KEMALIST SECULARISM   163

Bibliography   166
Index   179

CHRONOLOGY

ca. 570   Birth of Muhammad.

ca. 610   Muhammad's initial revelation.

ca. 613   The Prophet commences public preaching.

619   Crisis faced by Muhammad following death of his wife, Khadija, and of his uncle-protector, abu-Talib.

622   Hegira of Muhammad and about seventy followers from Mecca to Medina. Start of year 1 of the Islamic calendar.

624   Victory of Muslims over a larger Meccan ·force at Badr.

628   End of prolonged war between Byzantine and Sasanid empires. Exhaustion of both favors rapid Muslim expansion at their expense.

630   Muslims occupy Mecca.

632   Death of Muhammad.

632–661   First four caliphs: the Rashidun ("righteous").

ca. 652   First authoritative text of the Koran.

656–661   Caliphate of Ali, Muhammad's first cousin and son-in-law. Islamic capital shifted from Medina to Kufa (Iraq); instability caused by rebellion of Umayyad governor of Syria and by Kharijite agitation.

661–750   Umayyad caliphate, with capital at Damascus.

680   October 10 (10th of Moharram)—martyrdom of Ali's son, Hussein, at Karbala. Date becomes major Shiite anniversary.

691   Dome of the Rock constructed in Jerusalem.

711   Muslim force crosses Strait of Gibraltar to begin the "Moorish" conquest of Spain.

717–718   Muslim threat to eastern Europe subsides
           after failure of Arab siege of Byzantium.

732   Muslim threat to western Europe contained
           when Franks turn back Moorish force at
           Poitiers.

750   Abbasid "revolution," ending the Umayyad
           caliphate; capital subsequently transferred
           to Baghdad.

756   Independent Umayyad emirate at Cordova
           in Spain. Unity of Abbasid caliphate further
           eroded later in century by independence of
           Morocco and Tunisia.

767   Death of patron jurist of the Hanafi pathway
           of the Shari'a.

785   Construction started on Great Mosque of
           Cordova.

786–809   Harun ar-Rashid, caliph at Baghdad. Pres-
           tige of Abbasid Empire at zenith.

796   Death of patron jurist of the Maliki pathway
           of the Sharia.

813–833   Mamun, caliph at Baghdad. House of Wis-
           dom promotes translations from the Greek
           and encourages theological speculation.

820   Death of ash-Shafii, the most famous of
           early Muslim jurists, exponent of the legal
           pathway bearing his name.

836   Abbasid capital removed to Samarra for half
           a century.

ca. 840   Death of al-Khuwarizmi, expert mathema-
           tician.

855   Death of patron jurist of the fundamentalist
           Hanbali legal pathway.

870   Death of al-Bukhari, expert on hadiths.

873   At Samarra twelfth Shiite imam goes into
           concealment.

880   Ibn-Tulun mosque in Cairo.

897   Zaidi imamate established in Yemen.

909   Ismailian "hidden imam" proclaimed Mahdi and first caliph of the Fatimid line.

ca. 923 Death of ar-Razi, physician, skeptic, musician.

929   Number of caliphates increased to three when Umayyad emir of Cordova assumes the title. Carmathians capture Mecca.

935   Death of Abul-Hasan al-Ashari, who used Hellenic rationalism to buttress Islamic orthodoxy.

950   Death of al-Farabi, philosopher and musical theorist.

969   Capital of Fatimid caliphate transferred from Tunisia to Cairo. Foundation there of the mosque-university of al-Azhar.

1001   Ghaznawid Turks begin conquest of northwestern India.

1021   Fatimid caliph Hakim vanishes at Cairo. Hakim venerated as hidden imam by the Druzes.

1037   Death of Avicenna, the "universal man" of medieval Islam.

1056   Berber conquest of Black Empire of Ghana gives Muslims first foothold in sub-Saharan Africa.

1071   Byzantium defeated by Seljuk Turks, now at peak of their power.

1085   Christians reconquer Toledo, intellectual and scientific center of Moorish Spain.

1092   Assassins slay Nizam al-Mulk, chief minister of Seljuk sultans.

1099   First Crusade takes Jerusalem.

1111   Death of al-Ghazali, articulate defender of Sufism and orthodoxy.

1123   Death of Omar Khayyam, astronomer, poet, and (perhaps) Sufi.

1166	Death of the founder of the Qadiriya Sufi brotherhood.
1171	Saladin's conquest of Cairo: end of Fatimid caliphate.
1187	Saladin recaptures Jerusalem.
1198	Death of Averroes, Malikite judge and champion of Aristotelianism.
1204	Death of Averroes's disciple Maimonides, major figure in both the Jewish and the Islamic traditions.
1258	Baghdad taken by the Mongols. End of the Abbasid caliphate.
1273	Death of Jalal ud-din Rumi, Persian poet and mystic, founder of the Mevlevi dervishes.
1276	Death of Ahmad al-Badawi, saintly founder of the rustic Ahmadiya dervishes in Egypt.
1290	Muslim merchants from India secure first missionary base in Indonesia.
1389	Death of founder of Naqshbandi dervishes.
ca. 1400	Beginning of successful Muslim missions on the Malay peninsula.
1406	Death of ibn-Khaldun, jurist and philosopher of history.
1453	Capture of Byzantium by the Ottoman Turks.
1492	Christian capture of Granada, last Moorish stronghold in Spain.
1520–1566	Suleiman the Magnificent, emperor at Isstanbul: zenith of Ottoman power and culture (mosques designed by Sinan and embellished with Iznik tiles).
1556–1658	Empire of the Turkish Mogul dynasty at its height in India: Red Fort and Taj Mahal at Agra.
1587–1629	Abbas the Great, Safavid Shah of Iran and monumental rebuilder of Isfahan.

1792   Death of the founder of the Wahabi move-
            ment, puritanical response to Sufi excesses.

1840   Thomas Carlyle's lecture, "The Hero as
            Prophet," expressing a sympathetic under-
            standing of Muhammad.

1844   Millennium of the disappearance of the
            twelfth imam: In Persia the Bab declared
            to be the Mahdi and hidden imam, fore-
            runner of the Bahai faith.

1869   Opening of Suez Canal, symbol of Western
            imperialist supremacy.

1897   Death of al-Afghani, controversial exponent
            of Pan-Islam.

1905   Death of Muhammad Abduh, Egyptian ad-
            vocate of Islamic modernism.

1905–1906   Revolution in Persia, inaugurating long
            struggle to modernize the monarchy and
            end European imperialist controls.

1924   Turkish Republic abolishes the caliphate
            and abandons the Sharia. Kemalist secularist
            revolution in full swing.

1928   Foundation of the Muslim Brotherhood in
            Egypt.

1947   Partition of Indian subcontinent into pre-
            dominantly Muslim Pakistan and the largely
            Hindu Republic of India.

1949   Indonesia independent of Dutch colonial
            rule.

1950   Muslim resentment of Kemalist secularism a
            significant factor in Turkish election.

1952   January 26—Black Saturday in Cairo: anti-
            Western riots. July 23–26—Egyptian revolu-
            tion ending the monarchy and bringing
            Colonel Nasser to power.

1953   Death of ibn-Saud, founder of modern Saudi
            Arabian kingdom.

1958   July 14—revolution in Baghdad ends the Iraqi monarchy.

1965   Muslim officers and students thwart a communist coup in Indonesia.

1969   Overthrow of monarchy in Libya.

Important Annual Dates in the Islamic Calendar

In each successive year after 1972, these dates will fall ten or eleven days earlier in the Christian calendar year.

Feast of the Sacrifice	January 27, 1972
Beginning of Islamic Year 1392	February 16, 1972
Tenth of Moharram (Shiites only)	February 25, 1972
Month of Ramadan	October 9 to November 7, 1972

MEDIEVAL ISLAMIC WORLD

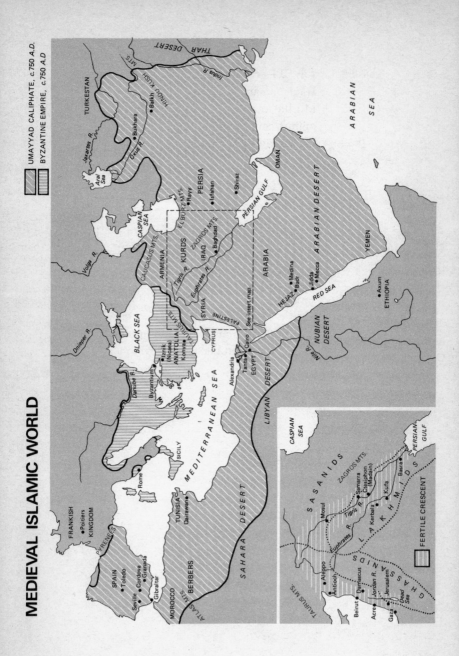

UMAYYAD CALIPHATE, c.750 A.D.

BYZANTINE EMPIRE, c.750 A.D.

FERTILE CRESCENT

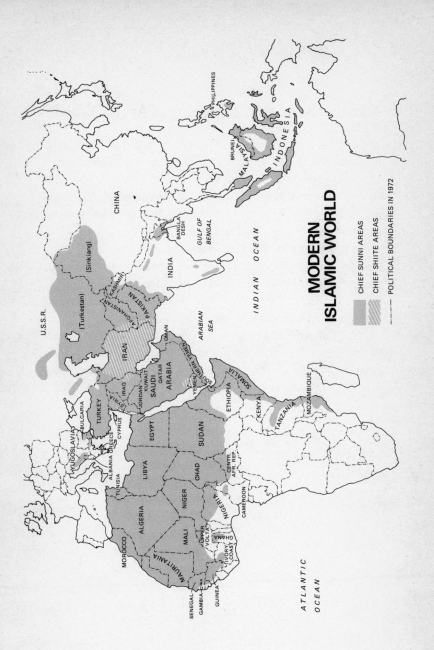

MODERN
ISLAMIC WORLD

CHIEF SUNNI AREAS
CHIEF SHIITE AREAS
POLITICAL BOUNDARIES IN 1972

U.S.S.R.

CHINA

(Sinkiang)

(Turkestan)

AFGHANISTAN

KASHMIR

PAKISTAN

INDIA

BANGLA DESH

GULF OF BENGAL

PHILIPPINES

BRUNEI

MALAYSIA

INDONESIA

INDIAN OCEAN

IRAN

IRAQ

SYRIA

JORDAN

KUWAIT

QATAR

OMAN

SAUDI ARABIA

YEMEN

SOUTHERN YEMEN

ARABIAN SEA

SOMALIA

ETHIOPIA

KENYA

TANZANIA

MOZAMBIQUE

TURKEY

CYPRUS

GREECE

ALBANIA

BULGARIA

YUGOSLAVIA

EGYPT

SUDAN

LIBYA

TUNISIA

CHAD

NIGER

CENTR. AFR. REP.

CAMEROON

NIGERIA

ALGERIA

MALI

UPPER VOLTA

GHANA

IVORY COAST

GUINEA

MAURITANIA

MOROCCO

SENEGAL

GAMBIA

ATLANTIC OCEAN

Author's Note on the Spelling of Arabic Words

Following present-day scholarly practice, this book uses the spellings *Muslim* and *Muhammad,* which come closer to approximating the sounds of the Arabic originals than do the traditional *Moslem* and *Mohammed.* Yet they are only approximations, for Arabic has no true vowels in its alphabet and also has several consonants that sound quite unlike any in English. Most systems of transliterating Arabic words into English involve accents or diacritical marks baffling to the lay reader who has no acquaintance with the Semitic languages. For these reasons, except for *Muslim* and *Muhammad,* this book retains older English spellings of Arabic words, which tend to be more familiar to the reader than transliterations that are technically more accurate. One feels more at home with *Mecca* than with *Makka,* and with the *Koran* rather than the *Qur'an.*

EDITOR'S INTRODUCTION

With the fall of the western half of the Roman Empire, at the hands of Germanic barbarians in the fifth century of the Christian Era, the center of organized power in the Mediterranean Basin passed eastward, to Byzantium with its capital in Constantinople (modern Istanbul). During the late fifth century and throughout the sixth, a series of capable Byzantine rulers and military commanders tried to restore the unity of Roman imperial rule. Extensive campaigns, costly in both men and resources, were fought in the Balkans, the Fertile Crescent, Italy, and western North Africa. And for a while, under the Emperor Justinian (527–565), it appeared as if the Empire would be restored and the Mediterranean Sea turned once more into a "Roman lake."

Within a century, however, the project of restoring Roman imperial rule had turned into little more than a dream. The pressures exerted from the north by the Slavs and from the east by a restored Persian Empire made it necessary for the Byzantines to concentrate on consolidating their power in the Anatolian peninsula (modern Turkey). Gradually, older centers of Roman power in Syria, Palestine, Egypt, North Africa, and ultimately, Italy, slipped from Byzantine hands. Then, in the late seventh century, a new contender for the title of successor to Rome as ruler of the world appeared on the historical scene. This new power was the Arabs, a people inspired by a new faith, Islam, which contended with Christianity itself as the spiritual cement of a new world community.

In his contribution to our series, John B. Christopher, professor of history at the University of Rochester, brilliantly summarizes the history of this new power and has analyzed the principal elements of this new faith. His assignment was a particularly difficult one, for unlike some of the major traditions with which this series has dealt, the evolution of Islam has not been characterized by a consistent movement toward the kind of political consolidation that marked, for example, Byzantium and Western Europe during the Middle Ages. In both of the latter cultures, religion and politics developed in tandem. Religious ideals were often at odds with the principal representatives of power, but the former always had the instrument of a unified state to *develop against* or, conversely, to *appeal to* for aid when threatened by contending religions or the possibility of disintegrating into radical sectarianism. In Islam, however, no such consistent development of a unified state occurred; its history has been a protracted story of internal division and sectarian strife. And as a result, much of Muslim history must be seen as a quest for the principle by which a host of sects, groups, and authorities might be judged and unification of those who affirm the faith might be achieved. At least, such a quest appears to be the principal problem facing the leaders of Muslim states today, caught as they are between pressures from without, exerted by the superpowers of Asia and the West, and from within, represented by their tendency to fragment and divide.

In his survey of the Islamic tradition, Christopher strikes a happy balance between representation of the components of Islam and analysis of its internal dynamics, which gives to the Muslim world its uniqueness as a contemporary cultural phenomenon. He tactfully distinguishes between the vital inner core of Muslim religious beliefs, which claim the devotion of one-sixth of the world population, and the multiplicity of forms that this devotion takes at different times and places in history. He amply records the fascinating diversity of thought, expression, and practice that Islam has promoted throughout the world since the death of the religion's founder, the Prophet Muh-

hamad, in A.D. 632. Christopher also assesses Islam's potentialities for promoting cultural unity and political rebirth
in the Arab world in our own time.

The main purpose of the book is "to correct and
sharpen the focus" of what Christopher calls the Western
images of Islam, one "heroic," the other "disparaging." The
contrast between the two images, he notes, derives from the
fact that Islam has had a genuinely heroic age, represented by the great cultural achievements of its medieval
period. During this heroic age, Islam expanded its power
from the Arabian peninsula eastward into Persia and westward into Spain. This expansion was attended by the fusion
of the original doctrines of the Prophet Muhammad with
the ideals and values of older centers of civilization, thereby
laying the foundations for that brilliant cultural flowering
that the Muslim world continues to draw on for inspiration
and for its unique sense of cultural self-identity in our
own time. But if this process of cultural fusion contrib-
uated to the brilliance of Muslim high civilization, it also
provided the occasion for political and religious division
within Islam. It is this tendency toward internal division
and sectarian strife that provides the basis for the other,
disparaging image of the Islamic tradition. Christopher
seeks to qualify the presuppositions of both images and,
in the process, provides us with a balanced view of Islam's
achievements and its potentialities for the future.

The first half of Christopher's book concentrates on
the foundations of Islam. In sections two through five, the
author analyzes the career and original doctrines of the
Prophet, especially as given in Islam's holy book, the Koran;
and in section six he indicates the implications of those
doctrines for the ordering of a specifically Muslim conception of the way to holiness. Here we can perceive the
similarities and differences between Islam and the two
other "religions of the book," Judaism and Christianity,
which place an equal stress on the necessity of the indi-

vidual quest for transcendental redemption. At the same time, we are permitted to see the extent to which the very cosmopolitanism of Islam, its capacities for addressing itself to problems indigenous to the areas in which it had spread, served the cause of political division and religious sectarianism. In the section titled "Orthodoxy and Heterodoxy," Christopher attempts to bring order into the Western conception of Islam as a house of many mansions, within which all of the faithful may claim a place in spite of the differences that might separate one group from another over points of doctrine and practice.

The principal problem which faced Islam after the death of the prophet was that of determining the locus of authority among the faithful. Islam is the individualistic creed par excellence. In this it resembles Judaism and some forms of Protestant Christianity, which also invest authority for determining the way of salvation in the individual believer, rather than in a specific caste or group such as a priesthood or a head of state. In Islam the final authority resides ultimately in the book, the Koran, which, like any book cast in poetic and allegorical language, lends itself to as many interpretations as there are interpreters. This in turn promotes the proliferation of contending sects and groups, each claiming for itself the discovery of the "true" or "essential" meaning of the complex patterns of imagery in which the sacred doctrine is presented.

This centrality of the sacred book to the whole religious endowment of Islam and the flexibility of the Arabic language in which it is written have promoted the development of a highly sophisticated *verbal* culture, in which subtlety of interpretation and sensitivity to poetic nuance are held in especially high esteem. This verbal virtuosity in turn has set a distinctive mark on Muslim civilization. Islam has excelled in the promotion of those aspects of thought and expression in which the word has the dominant place, in philosophy, science, and literature. Excellence in verbal expression accounts for the marvelous diversity within a unity of shared spiritual values that is so difficult for the Westerner to appreciate, trained as he is to see poetry and science as *opposed* forms of consciousness. But this diversity is as manifest as the unity that underlies it; and the question that many modern Muslims must face is whether or not, in an age of ideological strife, it may be crippling or fatal.

In the latter part of his book, Christopher gives examples of and analyzes the rich cultural heritage of medieval Islam and sets this heritage over against the problems of social and political organization with which it is asked to contend in the modern age. These sections provide the groundwork for the closing section in which the author considers the challenge of modernization and assesses the threat to Muslim cultural integrity that the age of ideology offers to the heirs of the Prophet.

In the section titled "The Modern Challenge," Christopher stresses the fact that the Islamic tradition is for the most part "a product of the Middle Ages." His analysis seems to suggest that the Muslim world of the present day can only modernize at the expense of its most highly valued cultural ideals. The Muslim dilemma is illustrated by the ambivalent relationship that exists between nationalistically inspired Muslim peoples, on the one hand, and the Soviet Union, dedicated to promotion of radically secular and internationalist ideals, on the other. A socialist political program appears to many Muslim leaders as the only way of projecting their peoples into a condition of modernity; these leaders feel that they must reconstitute their nations if they are to survive. And they are inclined to see their situations as similar to those of Russia on the eve of World War I. Modernization also implies expulsion of the Westerners who, since the imperialist period, have come to stand for disruptive meddling in Third World affairs. This makes of them natural allies of Soviet com-

munists, whose affirmed enemies are these same imperialist
states. A consistent socialist or communist program, however, must inevitably strike deep at the most revered principles of Islamic culture, principles in the interest of which
the efforts at modernization for survival have been under-
taken in the first place.

Christopher stresses that the Western powers, in
their dealings with Muslim states in the Near and Far
East, are probably correct in assuming that Islam is in-
herently hostile to communism. At the same time, he
suggests, for the Muslim peoples modernization through
Westernization may be no more acceptable than modernization through communization. Both would constitute a threat
to the cultural integrity in the interests of which national-
ization is being promoted. Like many of the older Western
European states, then, the Muslim world is caught between two ways to modernization, neither of which is
acceptable without reservations. As a result, the contemporary Muslim world is divided, not only over ends, but over
means as well. As a means, modernization can serve many
different purposes, among which is the strengthening of the
cultural identity that Islam represents for about one-sixth
of the world's populaton. If, however, the implementation
of the means threatens the end envisaged, the question is
raised as to whether the means themselves are to be
utilized. As a result many Muslim intellectuals and political
leaders are inclined to opt for a radical rupture with the
entire tradition of Islamic civilization. But this option remains empty as long as the masses continue to hold firm
to the faith of their fathers. Whether Islam has the resources to address itself to the problems posed by modernization is the crucial question for the future. Christopher's
book illuminates this question clearly, and gives us glimpses
of some of the answers that are likely to be given to it in
the immediate future of the Islamic world.

                                        Hayden V. White

INTRODUCTION:
TWO IMAGES
OF ISLAM

To almost all of us, even to agnostics and anticlericals, the Judeo-Christian tradition seems familiar, if only as part of our heritage and environment. To almost all of us the Islamic tradition appears, by contrast, strange and remote, the unfamiliar beliefs and customs of unfamiliar peoples. Thus it is hardly surprising that Europeans and Americans generally have a distorted image of Islam that does the Muslims less than justice by conveying the impression that their faith must be inferior to Judaism and Christianity.

What are the main components of the conventional Western image of Islam? Doubtless the best known fact about Islam is that a Muslim is permitted to have several wives, and from this it presumably follows that Islam must be more primitive than the monogamous religions. Though we no longer identify Muhammad with the Devil, as our medieval forbears did, the usual Western view of the Prophet is scarcely flattering. He is often pictured as an all too human adventurer, who imposed on the credulity of his followers and made religion the excuse for indulging his sexual appetite and securing his personal advancement. And from this it follows that, because Muhammad's own life was so much less saintly than that of Jesus, the religion he preached must be shallow and insincere as compared with Christianity. Thus, it is widely believed in the West that, although Muslim warriors of the past fought bravely in holy wars, they fought not to propagate their faith but only to insure themselves eternity in paradise, which with its wine and its dancing girls is much more fleshly than the Christian heaven. It is also believed that the average Muslim today satisfies his spiritual needs by the rote performance of prayer ritual, devoting neither thought nor feeling to his faith but merely accepting the fatalistic maxim—It is the will of Allah.

In the conventional Western image, Islam appears as a passive and static faith, alien to our concepts of progress and development, and suitable perhaps for conservative peasants and nomads but hardly for modern urban societies. Some American and European intellectuals, while accepting this disparaging estimate of present-day Islam, project another and very different image of the past Islamic world, endowing medieval Muslims with the magical qualities of culture heroes. According to this second image, Islamic cities from Persia to Spain created a wonderful and exotic civilization that made a substantial and inadequately acknowledged contribution to the culture of the Christian West. The contribution of Muslim scientists is suggested by the fact that we still employ Arabic numerals and use many words derived from Arabic, such as *alcohol, algebra, alkali, cipher, zenith,* and *zero*.[1] The contribution of Muslim navigators is suggested by terms of Arabic origin such as *monsoon* and *admiral* (that is, *amir al-bahr,* commander of the sea), and that of merchants by *check, tariff, sugar, orange, saffron,* and still other examples in which both the

[1] The prefix *al-* (sometimes transliterated *el-* or *ul-*) is the definite article in Arabic. Before words beginning with a *d, n, r, s,* or *t* sound the *l* is assimilated to the following consonant, and the spelling of the prefix may then be changed, as in Harun ar-rashid (rather than al-rashid) or Salah ad-din (rather than al-din).

thing and its name originated in the Islamic world. Muslim architects developed the pointed arch and the stone tracery called arabesque, both of which were later adapted for European Gothic buildings. Love poems from Muslim Spain stimulated the revival of secular poetry in twelfth-century France, and from further east came the uninhibited tales of *The Arabian Nights* that inspired Boccaccio and Chaucer. Last, and most important, the Western intellectual revival of the twelfth and thirteenth centuries might never have occurred at all if medieval Muslim philosophers had not preserved ancient Greek texts and written commentaries on them.

Both the disparaging image and the heroic image are somewhat out of focus. The former suffers from a kind of nearsightedness and fails to see that the range of Muslim religious experience extends far beyond the Western stereotype of the faithful performing their prayer routine or reciting memorized passages from the Koran. A visitor to one of the great mosques—al-Azhar in Cairo, the Dome of the Rock in Jerusalem, the Umayyad in Damascus, the Suleimaniye in Istanbul, or the Islamic Center in Washington—finds many evidences of the beauty and the richness of detail surrounding the faith. The heroic image suffers from farsightedness, the result of viewing the medieval Muslim world through a romantic haze. Some of the contributions credited to medieval Muslims were actually the work of Jews, Christians, or other non-Muslims, and many were borrowed from older cultures—Greek, Byzantine, Persian, or Indian. Arabic numbers, for example, might more appropriately be called Hindi, since the Arabs adapted them from an Indian invention, and some of the tales in *The Arabian Nights* also originated in India.

The main purpose of this book is to correct and sharpen the focus of Western images of Islam by adjusting them more sensitively to historical realities. Although it is difficult for a non-Muslim to comprehend or appreciate

the full character of Islam, it is not difficult to take the
first steps that will lead toward a partial understanding by
agreeing that just because Islam is so different from familiar
religions, it is not necessarily either superior or inferior to
them.

THE ARABIAN
SETTING

Many Westerners assume that the Judeo-Christian and Islamic traditions arose in very different settings. Westerners know that the former emerged among the shepherds, farmers, and townspeople who lived in the Fertile Crescent, the green belt arching from Palestine along the Mediterranean and across the top of the Syrian desert into the Euphrates and Tigris valleys. This corridor between the Egyptian and Mesopotamian "cradles of civilization" had itself been civilized for many centuries before the appearance of the Jews or of Jesus. On the other hand, Arabia at the time of Muhammad, about A.D. 600, is assumed to have been on the outer margins of civilization, a desert land peopled mainly by Bedouins still living in a precivilized state. From this assumption is derived the Western stereotype of Muhammad and his followers as near-barbarians, culturally much inferior to the founding fathers of Judaism and Christianity.

The assumption and the stereotype are both inaccurate. The Arabian peninsula is not made up entirely of barren desert, nor was it in Muhammad's day inhabited entirely by Bedouins[1] and cut off from the prosperous and cultivated Mediterranean world. In the southwestern corner

---

[1] The term *bedouin* is derived from the Arabic word for *desert* and describes the nomads of the North African, Arabian, and Syrian deserts.

of the peninsula, the well-watered highlands of Yemen had
long supported a settled farming population and had become a stake in international power politics. Further
north, the two centers most intimately identified with
Muhammad—Mecca and Medina—were by no means iso-
lated backwaters.

Mecca and Medina

Mecca lies in a hot, rocky valley, about forty-five
miles from the Red Sea, in the rugged western Arabian
area of the *Hejaz,* a term that means *barrier,* the barrier
between the coast and the deserts of the interior. The
original settlement grew up around a shrine focused on a
sacred black stone, perhaps a meteorite, which, according
to tradition, was delivered to earth by the angel Gabriel
and was placed in the cubical structure known as the
Kaaba by Abraham or possibly even by Adam himself.
The shrine was so important that the Bedouins observed a
three-month annual truce in their tribal warfare so that
pilgrims might worship and make sacrifices at the Kaaba.
Because neither the pilgrim traffic nor the meager farm
produce of the area was sufficient to support the population, the people of Mecca increasingly took advantage of
the fact that their little city lay on the caravan route between Yemen and the Fertile Crescent. Because of the
hazards of navigating the Red Sea, the parallel overland
route was used to convey both the incense of South Arabia
and the spices, textiles, jewels, and ivory brought to Yemen
by sea from India and Africa; caravans returning from Gaza
or Damascus carried articles made by Mediterranean craftsmen. Meccan merchants nursed this trade into a big business: one of their caravans, returning home from Gaza in
A.D. 624, is said to have numbered almost a thousand
camels. Consequently, seventh-century Mecca was the

largest town in Arabia; and many of its citizens had direct experience with the more advanced culture of the Fertile Crescent.

About 250 miles north of Mecca was the community of Yathrib, which consisted of a group of fortified farming villages scattered among the date palms and grain fields of an oasis covering 20 square miles. Later the Muslims changed the community's name to Medina, Arabic for *city*, the reference being to the city of the Prophet. Along with several other oases in the northern Hejaz, Yathrib included among its inhabitants a considerable number of Jews, some of whom were native converts to Judaism, whereas others were most probably the descendants of refugees from Babylonian or Roman persecution in Palestine. The refugees had apparently brought with them improved skills in agriculture and in goldsmithing and other crafts. At both Mecca and Medina, then, Muhammad lived not among changeless nomads but among settled people whose basic institutions were undergoing processes of change and crisis.

Arabs and Semites

The people of the Hejaz were in the great majority *Arabs*—a term that requires careful definition. Today Arab is used to designate those who speak Arabic, who claim the Arabian peninsula as their present or ancestral home, and who share in the sense of political kinship we know as Arab nationalism. The term does not refer to a specific religious group, for there are non-Muslim minorities in the Arab world; nor does it refer to a specific race, for Arabia and the Fertile Crescent have been human melting pots since the dawn of history. Nor is there any necessary racial connotation in the more inclusive term, *Semitic*, which has no real scientific basis and was invented in the modern West to describe the descendants of Shem, the

eldest son of Noah in the modern Book of Genesis. The
bonds that tie Arabs together and link them to other
Semitic peoples are more linguistic than racial.

In ancient times there were many Semitic languages
in the Fertile Crescent and adjoining areas. The most
notable was Aramaic, the mother tongue of Jesus, which
was very widely spoken until it was supplanted by Arabic
after the Muslim conquests. Today Aramaic survives mainly
as the fossilized liturgical language of Syriac used by some
of the Eastern churches, and only Arabic and Hebrew remain in use by large numbers of people. Although the
original homeland of the Semitic-speaking peoples is unknown and their early history is obscure, some of them
appeared in the Arabian peninsula long ago, perhaps about
3000 B.C. or even before. Some of them apparently moved
from Arabia to the greener lands of Egypt and the Fertile
Crescent prior to 2000 B.C.; the Hebrews and Aramaeans
followed later, and later still the Arabs themselves. Thus
the Arabs may be described historically as the most recent
and most successful in a long series of Semitic emigrants.

Language and Poetry

Language has long occupied an exceptionally important place in Arab history. In pre-Islamic days Arabic
was treasured as the finest expression of Bedouin genius;
later language was venerated by Muslims, both Arab and
non-Arab, as the medium of religious revelation and today
it is the cement of Arab nationalism. Another distinctive
feature of Arabic is the extraordinary richness of its vocabulary, for it can build whole families of words on a single
root of three consonants by a process of shifting the inter-
vening vowel sounds and adding prefixes and suffixes. From
the root *slm*, for example, are derived *salaam* ("peace or
safety"), *Islam, Muslim,* the proper name *Suleiman,* and a

dozen other words all associated with the idea of security or submission.

Arabic, like Hebrew, is written from right to left (numbers, however, run the other way), and pages are assembled backwards, or so it seems to us. Arabic letters bear little resemblance to our roman ones, though both may be traced back to the alphabet devised in Phoenicia more than three thousand years ago. Arabic letters, with their curving lines, their loops and neat little dots, lend themselves readily to elegant calligraphy—witness the very decorative effect of the Koranic passages so frequently embellishing mosques. It was the necessity of having an accurate text of the Koran that mothered the invention of the first full Arabic script in the seventh century. Even so, written Arabic may appear strange to us, because it has no capital letters and no punctuation marks and customarily records only the long vowels (the short ones must be figured out from the context).

Yet even before Muhammad and the Koran, Arabic literature had already produced magnificent poems, which were recited from memory rather than written down. The pre-Islamic poetry of the sixth century dealt with themes rather like those of the *Iliad*, the Old Testament, and other epics of an early heroic age. The poet described the beauties and terrors of nature, boasted of the virtues of his own tribe, and disparaged other tribes. Able to hold an audience of warriors spellbound, the poet combined the functions of magician, priest, and historian. As a medieval Arab scholar explained:

> When there appeared a poet in a family of the Arabs, the other tribes round about would gather together to that family and wish them joy of their good luck. . . . For a poet was a defence to the honour of them all, a weapon to ward off insult from their good name, and a means of perpetuating their glorious deeds and of establishing their

fame for ever. And they used not to wish one another
joy but for three things—the birth of a boy, the coming
to light of a poet, and the foaling of a noble mare.[2]

Later generations came to regard the pre-Islamic poems
as models to be learned by heart and to be imitated, but
not to be surpassed or even matched. These poetic traditions help to account for Muslim zeal in memorizing and
reciting the Koran, and they also help to explain the formal-
istic and changeless aspects of Islamic culture. When one
cannot improve on perfection, progress is an absurd idea.

The Shifting Balance of Power

The sixth and early seventh centuries, which formed
the golden age of Arabic poetry, were marked by a mounting crisis in political and social institutions. To understand
the nature of these critical changes and to visualize the
setting in which Islam arose, it is essential to correct the
oversimplified Western notion that the Arabian peninsula
has always been populated only by Bedouins who are iso-
lated from the outside world. The process of institutional
change affected the inhabitants of oasis and town more
than the Bedouins; this change was in turn much influenced by shifts in the balance of power both outside
and within the peninsula.

In the sixth century two powers dominated the
Middle East—the eastern Roman emperors of Byzantium,
who controlled Anatolia (Asia Minor), Syria, Palestine,
and Egypt; and the Sasanid emperors of Persia, whose
domains extended west of the present-day borders of Iran
and included the eastern sector of the Fertile Crescent in

[2] Ibn-Rashiq, *Ancient Arabian Poetry*, trans. C. J. Lyall
(Columbia University Press, 1930), p. xvii.

Mesopotamia. The two empires were traditional foes, and both sponsored buffer states on the frontier between the Fertile Crescent and the desert to deepen their defenses against one another and also to protect themselves against incursions by Arabs from the peninsula. The Byzantine buffer state, located in southern Syria, was organized by the Ghassanids, an Arab people who supplied soldiers to the Byzantine army in return for imperial subsidies. The Sasanid buffer state was organized by the Arab Lakhmids, who ruled territories to the south and west of the Euphrates.

The Ghassanids adopted the Aramaic language and accepted Christianity—not the Orthodox faith of Byzantium but the Monophysite heresy widespread in Syria and Egypt. Named from the Greek words for *single* and *nature*, the Monophysites rejected the doctrine of Christ's dual nature, at once human and divine. By stressing the divinity of Christ, at least in the eyes of their Orthodox opponents, they minimized the sacrifice of the human Jesus on the cross, thereby neglecting the central drama of Christianity. In accordance with a pattern very common in Middle Eastern history, this religious difference had momentous political results. It increasingly alienated the Monophysite Ghassanids from their Orthodox Byzantine patrons, promoting the disintegration of the Ghassanid buffer state and ultimately facilitating the Muslim conquest of the western Fertile Crescent.

In the eastern Fertile Crescent, too, religious tensions increased. The Lakhmids likewise were Christian heretics, in this case Nestorians, who occupied the opposite pole from the Monophysites, doctrinally speaking. Named for a theologian prominent in the fifth-century disputes over the nature of Christ, the Nestorians laid heavy stress on the humanity of Jesus and on his sacrifice. While the Nestorians won many converts in the Sasanid Empire, the Persian government continued to promote the old official

cult of Zoroastrianism. Another source of disaffection between the Lakhmids and their Persian patrons appeared at
the close of the sixth century when the Sasanid emperor
attempted to place Lakhmid lands under the direct rule
of his own officials. Again, the way was being prepared
for eventual conquest by the Muslims.

The two empires which might have thwarted that
conquest were weakened not only by internal dissensions
but also by their mutual conflict. In a prolonged Sasanid-
Byzantine war (A.D. 602–628), the first round went to the
Persians, who occupied the entire Fertile Crescent plus
Egypt. Yet they were unable to repel the raids made by
Bedouins from Arabia across the Euphrates frontier, which
the Lakhmids had once kept secure. The second round
went to the Byzantines, but at the cost of draining their
economy and their reserves of manpower. Heavy Byzantine
levies on the population of the western Fertile Crescent
further alienated the Syrians, particularly the large heretical
Monophysite and Nestorian communities. By the time of
Muhammad's prophetic mission both the Byzantine and
Sasanid empires were close to exhaustion.

Meantime, the focus of power was also shifting
within Arabia. The decline of Yemen, once the most prosperous region of the peninsula, was highlighted by the
collapse about A.D. 550 of the great Marib dike, which for
many centuries had irrigated crop lands in eastern Yemen
and was never to be repaired. Yemen had also become an
arena of competition between Jewish and Christian missionaries. When a Jewish king persecuted Christian Yemenis,
the latter sought help from the Byzantine emperor; he
transmitted their appeal to the Christians of Ethiopia, who
were the descendants of South Arabian emigrants to Africa.
Thus it was that Yemen underwent a half century of
Ethiopian occupation, which ended between A.D. 570 and
A.D. 580, when the Persians moved in and made Yemen a
loosely held outpost of the Sasanid Empire.

The Ascendancy of Mecca

Mecca was the chief beneficiary of the changing power constellation. Because of the disorder in the Lakhmid and Ghassanid borderlands of Arabia, shippers abandoned the passage from India to the Mediterranean via the Persian Gulf, the Euphrates valley, and Syria and utilized instead the route through the Hejaz paralleling the Red Sea. The merchants of Mecca took over the caravan trade that had once been organized by the Yemenis and reached their own favorable commercial arrangements with Byzantium, Persia, and Ethiopia.

The new prosperity and the new contacts with the wider world, however, severely strained the political and social fabric of Mecca. In the early seventh century the city was still governed by the rudimentary institutions appropriate for a community of former Bedouins but not for an expanding commercial town. The people of the desert were accustomed to acting collectively as members of a hierarchy of kinship groups—the family; the clan, grouping several families linked by blood ties; and the tribe, consisting of related clans. Vengeance, for example, was taken not by an aggrieved individual alone but by his family or clan or even tribe; the political decisions of clan or tribe were made by the *majlis*, the council of elders, rather than by the *sheik* or chieftain, who was often only a figurehead. In Mecca, where the population was still divided into clans, all belonging to the tribe of Quraish, the increasing wealth and power of individual merchants undermined the old structures of clan and *majlis* and the old traditions of collective action. Yet, since the new plutocrats managed to dominate the city without creating new administrative machinery, a kind of institutional vacuum characterized Meccan political life.

At the same time (about A.D. 600), social tensions also increased in Mecca, centered now less on traditional feuds between clans and more on economic rivalries. A rift was developing between the wealthy merchants, on the one hand, and the less successful small traders and workingmen, on the other. What was true in Mecca also characterized to some degree other parts of the Hejaz, wherever caravan trade, oasis farming, and settled communities were developing and dislocating traditional ways. The political and social institutions of the Arabs failed to keep pace with the forces of economic change. And so, too, did their religious institutions.

Pre-Islamic Religion

From time out of mind Arabs had worshiped the spirits believed to dwell in sacred springs, trees, and stones, such as the celebrated black stone in the Meccan Kaaba. They also believed in jinn, supernatural beings who assumed earthly form to interfere in the lives of men, sometimes benignly but more often maliciously. In addition, the Arabs came to venerate gods and goddesses rather like those of other peoples of antiquity, with a tribe fixing on one or more of these divinities as its own. Mecca was the center for the cult of three goddesses—al-Lat, al-Uzza, and Manat—revered by the Quraish and nearby tribes; in addition, the Kaaba, which attracted pilgrims from a much wider area, was said to house several hundred different idols.

Much evidence exists to suggest that by the sixth century many Arabs were beginning to find the old cults inadequate. Among some tribes the figure of the poet quite overshadowed that of the priest or soothsayer, and the yearning for a higher religion increased the appeal of Judaism and Christianity. Monophysites and Nestorians made many converts among Arab peoples like the Ghassanids and Lakhmids living close to the Fertile Crescent and also among Yemenis at the other extremity of the peninsula. Midway, at Mecca, a small but significant number of ascetics and seekers appeared, whom Muslims later called *hanifs*. Modern scholarship questions the traditional translation of *hanif* as *monotheist* and is also uncertain as to the extent, if any, that Christian or Jewish teachings may have influenced the *hanifs*. In any case, the Meccan *hanifs* seem to have been striving to elevate a single god above the welter of pagan deities. This was Allah, a name most probably derived from the Arabic *al-ilah,* which means *the god*.

By the opening of the seventh century an atmosphere of material and moral crisis was enveloping many parts of the Arabian peninsula. The old order seemed to be dissolving, and the new was powerless to be born. The time was ripe for a great innovator, a man who could bridge the gap between the old primitive ways of the desert and the more complex requirements of the settled commercial way of life and who could create the new institutions Arab society needed so desperately. This was the role filled so remarkably by Muhammad.

THE PROPHET

Muhammad was born, probably about the year A.D. 570, into a family of the Banu Hashim ("sons of Hashim"), a clan of Quraish that had played a prominent role in Meccan history, and from whom the Hashimite monarchs of twentieth-century Jordan and Iraq claim descent. The great Muslim biography of the Prophet, the Sira,[1] which dates from the eighth century, traced the ancestry of Muhammad back to Ishmael, son of Abraham in the Book of Genesis by the concubine Hagar. Muslims believe that Ishmael was the progenitor of the Arab people, whereas Isaac, the son born later to Abraham and his wife Sarah, was the progenitor of the Jewish people. Modern scholars reject the genealogy of Muhammad and many other details of the Sira as extravagant embellishments in the story-telling tradition of Arabic literature, but they accept its broad outlines as sound in the main. It is generally agreed that Muhammad's great-grandfather, for whom the Banu Hashim were named, pioneered in the caravan trade with Syria, and that Muhammad's grandfather had the important privilege of furnishing food and water to pilgrims visiting the Kaaba. His grandfather is also credited with having reconstructed the sacred well of Zamzam, the waters of which, according to legend, first appeared when the

[1] Sirat Rasul Allah ("Life of the Prophet of God"), written by ibn-Ishaq and edited by ibn-Hisham; there is an English translation by Alfred Guillaume, A Life of Muhammad (Oxford University Press, 1955).

16

angel Gabriel intervened to slake the thirst of Hagar and
Ishmael after Abraham had abandoned them at the in-
sistence of Sarah.

Muhammad's father died on a caravan journey, probably before his son was born; and the boy was brought up
by his grandfather and, after his death, by Muhammad's
uncle abu-Talib, the head of the Banu Hashim. At this
time the Banu Hashim, though still respected in Mecca,
had been surpassed in riches and influence by other clans.
Because Muhammad did not inherit wealth, he had to
make his own way; he apparently served as business agent
for Khadija, a well-to-do widow many years his senior,
whom he eventually married. The couple had six children,
and their marriage seems to have been outstandingly con-
genial; not until after Khadija's death, in A.D. 619, did
Muhammad follow Arab custom and take other wives.

The *Sira* claims that Muhammad made a journey to
Syria as Khadija's agent and also an earlier trip as a lad
accompanying a caravan of his uncle. These claims have
prompted much speculation and controversy as to whether
Muhammad must therefore have had some kind of direct
experience with Syrian Christianity. But it cannot be proved
that Muhammad ever traveled to Syria, and it is the consensus of scholars that, although he was aware of Christianity and Judaism, his knowledge was general and vague,
based on hearsay, on the second-hand reports circulating
in Mecca. There is no evidence that he had any first-hand
acquaintance with Jewish or Christian worship or with
the Bible. Indeed, Muslim tradition holds that Muhammad
was illiterate, in spite of the fact that one would expect a
business agent to have had some ability to read and write.

It is conjectured that Muhammad's religious views
may have been influenced to a considerable degree by the
hanifs, who were very critical of the pagan practices and
low moral tone of Meccan society. Recent scholarship,

particularly Montgomery Watt's study, *Muhammad at Mecca* (Oxford University Press, 1953), stresses the significance of his personal concern over the city's increasing commercialism and materialism. Muhammad is thought to have participated in the League of the Virtuous, which linked the Banu Hashim and other less prosperous clans against attempts by the wealthy clans to exclude Yemenis from trade with Mecca. The issue here was partly economic, since the poorer clans depended on wares supplied by Yemenis for the conduct of their own little businesses. But a question of justice was also at stake, for the Yemeni merchants had a long-established and recognized position in Mecca.

The Call To Recite

As the years passed, Muhammad's sense of alienation from existing Meccan society evidently increased, and at times he retreated to a cave in a nearby mountain for meditation and prayer. During one retreat, probably about the year A.D. 610, when he was approximately 40 years old, he experienced the traumatic seizure or awakening that was to transform him into a prophet. In a dream or vision Muhammad saw a heavenly being, who may have been the angel Gabriel, he later suggested, or possibly even Allah himself. The being commanded Muhammad to recite certain messages and, when Muhammad at first refused, struggled with him until he agreed to comply. And so Muhammad memorized and then repeated the messages to his family and some of his fellow citizens as divine revelations. Here is part of the first message:

> Recite: In the Name of thy Lord who created,
> created Man of a blood-clot.
> Recite: And thy Lord is the Most Generous,
> who taught by the Pen,
> taught Man that he knew not.

> No indeed: surely Man waxes insolent,
>   for he thinks himself self-sufficient.
> Surely unto thy Lord is the Returning.[2]

During the remaining years of his life Muhammad experienced a great many additional seizures and received a host of additional revelations, usually, he believed, through the angel Gabriel. The complete roster of revelations comprises the *Koran*, a word which means *recital* and has in Arabic a sacred connotation very like that of *scripture* in English.

Until recently many non-Muslims dismissed Muhammad's alleged religious experiences as the convulsions of an epileptic, or the outbursts of a hysterical person, or the fraudulent, self-induced episodes of an opportunist. In the light of modern medical and psychological knowledge, such views no longer appear very tenable. Epileptics, for example, have no memory of what has occurred during their attacks, whereas Muhammad gave vivid reports of what happened to him. Moreover, the very symptoms which used to be thought indicative of Muhammad's epilepsy are now considered quite compatible with intense religious excitement—convulsive movements during his seizures, foam on his lips, profuse sweating even on a cold day, complaints of hearing the clanking of chains or the ringing of bells. Do these symptoms suggest the delusions of hysteria? Most scholars today think not. It is conjectured that Muhammad seldom had visions after his initial experience, nor did he necessarily hear an actual voice relaying to him the full text of a divine message. Many a revelation apparently came to Muhammad as a sudden intuition, a flash of inspiration, an idea implanted by the angel Gabriel rather than a word-by-word communication.

The accounts of Muhammad's prolonged and anguished

[2] A. J. Arberry, *The Koran Interpreted*, II (Macmillan, 1955), sura 96, 345.

doubts over the source of his messages argue very strongly
in favor of his sincerity. The perpetrator of a fraud could
hardly have invented the crisis that engulfed Muhammad
after his first revelation, when, fearing that an evil jinni
had taken possession of him, he contemplated suicide. Sustained by the sympathy of Khadija, and gradually reassured
by further revelations, he became convinced after many
months had passed that he had indeed been chosen to be
the Prophet or messenger of Allah.

Preaching and Persecution in Mecca

About the year A.D. 613 Muhammad was sufficiently
sure of his vocation to commence public preaching in
Mecca. So far as we can learn from the early revelations
in the Koran, he denounced selfishness and materialism and
called on his fellow citizens to submit to Allah and surrender themselves to God's will—whence the terms *Islam*
("submission") and *Muslim* ("one who has submitted").
He repeated Allah's stern reminders of the impending Day
of Judgment:

> O thou shrouded in thy mantle,
>   arise, and warn!
> Thy Lord magnify
>   thy robes purify
> and defilement flee!
> Give not, thinking to gain greater
>   and be patient unto thy Lord.
> For when the Trump is sounded
>   that day will be a harsh day,
>   for the unbelievers not easy.[3]

As a reminder of the need for submission Muhammad began to lead the Muslims in the bowing, kneeling, and

[3] *Ibid.*, Sura 74, p. 310.

prostrations of the ritual prayers that have been a feature
of Islam ever since.

Who were the first Muslims, the first Meccans to
heed the urgent warnings relayed by Muhammad? Natu-
rally, they were not the richest men of the city, who dis-
liked Muhammad's strictures against their wealth and behavior; nor were they largely the poor and the outcast.
Many of his early followers came from the middle social
and economic level—leaders of less wealthy clans, young
men for the most part, and junior members of more successful clans. The number of Muslims at first remained
relatively small, so that the rich and powerful did not attempt any sustained or strenuous persecution. Inasmuch
as Mecca had neither a standing army nor a police force,
the security of the individual depended on the protection
of his clan; of this Muhammad was assured so long as his
uncle and guardian, abu-Talib, was chief of the Banu
Hashim.

A very critical moment arrived for him when abu-
Talib died, about A.D. 619, and leadership of the Hashimite
clan passed to another uncle of Muhammad, who was very
hostile to Islam and withdrew protection from the Prophet,
leaving him, in effect, an outlaw. The crisis was intensified
by the death of Khadija, which occurred at nearly the
same moment. Deprived of his two greatest champions,
Muhammad felt the full weight of the opposition to him
and within a year or two decided to quit Mecca. The *Sira*
describes his situation concisely and convincingly:

> When the Quraysh became distressed by the
> trouble caused by the enmity between them and the
> apostle and those of their people who accepted his teach-
> ing, they stirred up against him foolish men who called
> him a liar, insulted him, and accused him of being a
> poet, a sorcerer, a diviner, and of being possessed. How-
> ever, the apostle continued to proclaim what God had
> ordered him to proclaim, concealing nothing, and excit-

ing their dislike by condemning their religion, forsaking
their idols, and leaving them to their unbelief.[4]

Specifically, the Quarish feared that Muhammad would
jeopardize the traffic of pilgrims to the Kaaba and other
pagan shrines in the Hejaz, thus endangering the trade and
prosperity of the city and undermining its most cherished
traditions. They feared Muhammad as a revolutionary sub-
verter of the Meccan way of life.

Muhammad was indeed a revolutionary, whose
preaching altered not only men's religious beliefs and
practices but also the whole fabric of their existence. At-
tacking and discarding the old regime, he began to build
a new order in the cities and oases of the Hejaz, telling
the Arabs that they were part of something greater than a
medley of warring tribes and clans. This something was
the *umma*, the Muslim Arab community or nation—a concept that entitles Muhammad to be ranked as the first
Arab nationalist. The cementing force of his nationalism
was religion, for Islam was concerned with all the values
and activities of men, including their political organization
as well as their social and economic behavior. From the
start church and state were inseparable and identical in
the Muslim world. This identity characterized the *umma*
organized by Muhammad at Medina during the final decade
of his life.

The Decade at Medina

When he realized how perilous it was for him to
remain in Mecca, Muhammad began to plan carefully for
his departure. Finding that possible havens near Mecca
were insecure, he eventually picked Medina when about
seventy-five of its men invited him to come to their oasis
and pledged themselves to his defense. In A.D. 622, ac-

[4] Guillaume, *The Life of Muhammed,* p. 130.

cordingly, Muhammad secretly left Mecca with about seventy of his followers. This emigration is called the *Hegira* (*hijrah* comes closer to the pronounciation of the Arabic word), and it was a great event in Muslim history, marking the commencement of the year 1 of the Islamic calendar.[5]

To the men of Mecca Muhammad threatened an established way of life; to the men of Medina he offered the promise of easing their community's chronic tensions, which had been heightened by an influx of Bedouin and Yemeni immigrants. No individual or group had emerged in Medina capable of maintaining law and order in the face of the incessant feuds among rival Arab clans and their Jewish allies. When pilgrims from Medina visiting the Kaaba learned of Muhammad's preaching, they decided he might be the judge and arbiter they so sorely needed. Muhammad soon demonstrated that the seemingly ungovernable people of Medina could be governed under Islam and that the Muslim *umma* could win over most of the Arabs. By the time of his death, a decade after the Hegira, Muhammad was not only a venerated prophet and the founder of a new religion but also the uncrowned king of Arabia and the founder of a rapidly expanding empire.

Muhammad's success depended on his good fortune and on his talent for realistic politics as well as on the appeal of his preaching. When he arrived at Medina, he had the initial advantage of gaining at least passive acceptance from many, perhaps most, of its non-Jewish inhabitants. He relied chiefly, however, on the emigrants, the Meccans who had joined him in the Hegira. Deprived

[5] The letters A.H. after a year indicate that it is numbered according to the Islamic calendar, in which the year is made up of 12 lunar months, totaling 354 days. Thus, it takes 103 Muslim years to equal a Chirstian century, and the dates of the great Islamic religious festivals gradually move from season to season. The year 1390 A.H. began on March 9, 1970, 1391 A.H. on February 27, 1971, and 1392 A.H. on February 16, 1972.

of land and other means of support, the emigrants resorted to the Bedouin custom of seizing booty by raids on caravans and settlements. In those primitive days contemporaries seem to have accepted this activity as a fact of life. Muhammad gave the raiders a missionary quality by calling them "strivers" in the path of Allah; thus did *jihad*, the Arabic word for *striving*, acquire its Islamic connotation of a holy war.

In Muhammad's day the chief target of the jihad was the Quraish merchant oligarchy. For several years Medina and Mecca carried on intermittent warfare, beginning with emigrant raids on Quraish caravans and reaching a climax in the defeat of a Meccan contingent by a smaller force of Muslims in A.D. 624 at Badr, between Medina and the Red Sea. The victory demonstrated Muhammad's skill as a practical organizer and also vindicated his claim to be the spokesman chosen by Allah. Though the Meccans subsequently twice invaded the oasis of Medina, they were never able to deliver a knockout blow against Muhammad or recover the prestige lost at Badr. Soon, some of the chief warriors of Mecca were converted to Islam, and in A.D. 630 the Muslims occupied the city in an operation that was largely peaceful.

The contest between Muhammad and the Quraish greatly affected Muslim relations with the Jews and with the nomadic tribes of Arabia. At first Muhammad expected that the Jews of Medina would accept Islam, acknowledging his own revelations as the fulfillment of those brought earlier by the prophets of the Old Testament. In gestures to win Jewish support he directed Muslims to face toward Jerusalem during prayer and to observe the Jewish fast of Yom Kippur, the Day of Atonement. The Medinan Jews, however, rejected his claims to be a prophet and repudiated the idea that the Allah of Muhammad had any connection with their Jewish God. So Muhammad substituted daytime fasting during the month of Ramadan for

the observance of Yom Kippur and commanded worshippers
to face toward Mecca rather than Jerusalem. Arabia, not
Palestine, was to be the focus of Islam.

Although Muhammad preached toleration of Jews as
"People of the Book" because the Old Testament contained part of Allah's message to mankind, the Jewish
policy he practiced exhibited all the harshness of im-
memorial tribal custom. After the victory at Badr, he de-
ported one of the three major Jewish groups from Medina
and confiscated its property. The second group later suffered a similar fate; and because the third Jewish group
was reputed to be especially hostile to Islam, Muhammad
ordered the men killed and the women and children sold
into slavery. When the Muslims captured a populous
Jewish oasis eighty miles north of Medina, Muhammad
ordered that the lands be divided among his followers;
the Islamic commonwealth had acquired a colony. A con-
stant impetus toward further Islamic imperialism came from
Bedouin tribes who gave their allegiance to Muhammad
not so much out of conviction about the truth of his
preaching as out of awe at his success against the leaders
of Mecca. To overcome the restlessness of the new recruits,
who chafed under rules designed for settled communities,
Muhammad channeled Bedouin energies into the jihad.
The last years of his life were marked by Muslim expedi-
tions in the direction of the Fertile Crescent and the
frontiers of the Byzantine Empire.

Muhammad died in A.D. 632, soon after returning to
Medina from a solemn pilgrimage to Mecca, where he led a
large group of Muslims in making the circuit of the Kaaba
seven times and kissing its sacred black stone. By the
time of his death the religion that he founded had acquired
many of its most distinctive traits. It already demonstrated
the very positive missionary drive, warlike and expansionist, summed up in the word *jihad*. Islam already showed a
disposition to make an occasional concession to older re-

ligions by assimilating one or another of their practices. Muhammad continued to venerate the Kaaba and its stone, but he took care to cleanse the Kaaba of the hundreds of pagan idols it had formerly contained. Islam already had a particular identification not just with Mecca but with the Arabian peninsula, the Arabic language, and the Arab *umma*. Yet Islam's Arabism did not necessarily diminish its ecumenical appeal, for Muhammad was preaching to all mankind as well as to the Arabs. Allah is much, much more than a local, tribal, or national deity; he is the universal God.

THE TEACHINGS
OF ISLAM

The primary source of Islamic teachings is the Koran. To Muslims it is no mere book but the word of God as revealed to Muhammad, supplementing and completing the revelations of the early prophets and of Jesus; it contains in its entirety a truth of which only a part may be found in the Old Testament or the New. It is, a sympathetic Western expert notes,

> the holy of holies. It must never rest beneath other books, but always on top of them; one must never drink or smoke when it is being read aloud, and it must be listened to in silence. It is a talisman against disease and disaster. In many places children under ten years of age are required to learn by heart its 6200 odd verses. . . .
> There is something impressive and touching in the sight of simple people murmuring the sacred text as they travel. . . . Some people never leave their homes without having a small copy . . . on their person. The bereaved find their great consolation in reading it. No event of consequence passes without the reading of an appropriate passage.[1]

Recitation or chanting of selected verses is the closest Islamic approach to liturgy or to hymn-singing; and Koranic passages are much favored for the decoration of mosques, where the depiction of human beings or other living

[1] Alfred Guillaume, *Islam* (Penguin, 1954), p. 74.

creatures is forbidden. For Muslims the significance of the Koran is all-embracing, perhaps even surpassing that of the Bible for fundamentalist Christians.

The full text of the Koran, as we now have it, dates from about twenty years after Muhammad's death when it was pieced together, in the picturesque words of the traditional account, from "scraps of parchment and leather, tablets of stone, ribs of palm branches, camels' shoulder blades and ribs, pieces of board, and the breasts of men." By this time trained reciters had committed large portions of the Koran to memory, just as they were accustomed to do with the great poems of the sixth century. It is also probable that Muhammad himself had been so concerned with the accurate preservation of certain verses that he dictated them to secretaries.

Although there is little reason to suppose that the lag of twenty years before the completion of the Koran distorted the essence of Muhammad's message, the task of non-Muslim students of Islam has been complicated. The reasons why were admirably summarized more than a century ago by Thomas Carlyle, one of the first Western men of letters to attempt a fair-minded appraisal of Muhammad:

> Nothing but a sense of duty could carry any European through the Koran. We read in it, as we might in the State-Paper Office, masses of lumber, that perhaps we may get some glimpses of a remarkable man. It is true we have it under disadvantages: the Arabs see more method in it than we. Mahomet's followers found the Koran lying all in fractions, . . . and they published it, without any discoverable order as to time or otherwise; merely trying, . . . and this not very strictly, to put the longest chapters first. The real beginning of it, in that way, lies almost at the end: for the earliest portions were the shortest. Read in its historical sequence it perhaps would not be so bad. Much of it, too, they say is rhythmic; a kind of wild chanting song, in the original. This may be a great point; much perhaps has been lost

in the Translation here. Yet with every allowance, one feels it difficult to see how any mortal ever could consider this Koran as a Book written in Heaven, too good for the Earth; as a well-written book, or indeed as a *book* at all; and not a bewildered rhapsody.[2]

The 6200 verses of the Koran are grouped in 114 chapters or suras, which vary enormously in length, from a very few lines to more than thirty pages. As Carlyle complained, the arrangement of chapters by order of decreasing length places near the end the brief, early Meccan suras, which contain the most dramatic verses of the Koran. Another source of difficulty lies in the titles assigned to the suras, some of which bear little relation to their content; a famous example is sura 2, the longest of all, called "The Cow." Four suras are titled by one or more letters of the Arabic alphabet—*Ta, Ha, Ya, Sin, Sad, Qaf*—and a few others are prefaced by groups of letters after the title—*Alif, Lam, Mim, Ra,* and so on. The reasons for this remain a mystery; perhaps the solution lies in the ingenious suggestion that the disjointed letters represent Muhammad's stammering and mumbling efforts to articulate immediately after the traumatic experience of receiving a revelation (M. Rodinson, *Mohammed* (Pantheon, 1971), pp. 75, 93).

Muslims justify the unique structure of the Koran on the ground that it was prescribed by Muhammad himself. A leading Western convert to Islam finds a rationale for the placement of the early Meccan suras: "The inspiration of the Prophet progressed from inmost things to outward things, whereas most people find their way through outward things to things within."[3]

The early Meccan verses are indeed concerned with inmost things—the relationship of man and God, the im-

[2] Thomas Carlyle, "The Hero as Prophet," *On Heroes, Hero-Worship and the Heroic in History* (Oxford University Press [London], 1946), pp. 25–86.
[3] M. M. Pickthall, *The Meaning of the Glorious Koran: An Explanatory Translation* (Mentor, 1953), pp. xxviii–xxix.

minence of the Last Judgment—and are written in a crisp, rhyming prose that sounds like poetry. The verses from Medina are less poetic and more concerned with outward things, such as the administration of the *umma* and the day-to-day conduct of its members. The first Medinan suras, from the period immediately after the Hegira, include stories or parables from the Old and New Testaments, often in rather garbled form. As Muhammad's expectation of swift conversion of Jews and Christians faded, the later Medinan suras focused on Abraham, whom Muhammad called the "friend of God," because he was a pioneering *hanif* and preacher against the worship of idols. The Arabs and Jews, Muhammad believed, as descendants of Abraham through his sons Ishmael and Isaac, respectively, should fulfill their historic destiny by accepting Islam.

The Koran exemplifies in the highest degree the hypnotic qualities of early Arabic literature. In Muslim devotions the Koran is not read, in the conventional sense of the term, but recited or intoned in a fashion that stresses its poetic quality and its power to stir or grip the listener. Muslims tend to hold that it is improper—indeed, sacrilegious—to tamper with the traditional order or original language of the Koran. In deference to Muslim sensibilities some English versions bear such titles as *The Koran Interpreted* or *The Meaning of the Glorious Koran: An Explanatory Translation* to indicate that they cannot presume to be the actual words of God.[4] Other translations, however, attempt to make what Carlyle termed "a bewildered rhapsody" more intelligible to non-Muslim readers by arranging the suras and even individual verses in their proper chronological sequence.[5]

---

[4] Arberry, *The Koran Interpreted;* Pickthall, *The Meaning of the Glorious Koran.*

[5] Examples are J. M. Rodwell, *The Koran,* first published in 1861 (Everyman's Library, 1933); Richard Bell's scholarly dissection and reconstruction, *The Qur'an, Translated with a Critical Re-arrange-*

Hadiths

The Koran is not the sole source of direct information about Muhammad and his teachings. Reports of statements he had made and actions he had taken in everyday life were passed along by word of mouth from his companions to later generations; these statements are called *hadiths* or traditions. Although not claimed by Muslims to be the words of God, the hadiths have been endowed with a special importance since even the details of Muhammad's daily routine could reflect divine guidance. Many hadiths were incorporated into the *Sira*, the early biography of the Prophet (see p. 16); later, al-Bukhari (A.D. 810–870) issued a compendium of hadiths. Here is one of the thousands of traditions he included:

Muhammad ibn Muqatil Abu'l-Hasan has related to me saying: Abdallah informed us on the authority of Humaid ibn Abd ar-Rahman, on the authority of Abu Huraira—with whom may Allah be pleased—that a man came to the Apostle of Allah—upon whom be Allah's blessing and peace—saying: "O Apostle of Allah, there is no hope for me . . . I had intercourse with my wife during Ramadan." The Prophet answered: "Then set free a slave." Said he: "I have none." The Prophet answered: "Then fast for two months on end." Said he: "But I could not." The Prophet answered: "Then feed sixty poor people." Said he: "I have not the wherewithall." Just then there was brought to the Prophet a basket of dates, so he said to the man: "Take this and distribute it as charitable alms in expiation of your sin." Said he: "O Apostle of Allah, am I to distribute it to other than my own family? when by Him in whose hands is my soul there is no one between the gateposts of the city more needy than I am." Thereat the Prophet laughed till his

ment of the Surahs, 2 vols. (Edinburgh University Press, 1937; reprinted 1960); and N. J. Dawood's more readable, *The Koran: A New Translation* (Penguin, 1956).

canine teeth showed, and he said: "Go along and take it."[6]

This text suggests the almost insoluble problems surrounding the authenticity of hadiths transmitted orally over a span of more than two centuries. Perhaps the authorities cited were not reliable, perhaps one of them might have misquoted the Prophet, perhaps the whole hadith was forged by an interested party—no one could, or can, be entirely certain. Some alleged hadiths were obviously borrowed from the Old Testament or the New; some were edifying precepts devised by good Muslims to attract errant brethren back to the path of righteousness; and some were simply tall tales made up by storytellers to elicit generous tips from their audiences. Al-Bukhari is said to have examined 600,000 hadiths (another source says 300,000) and classified each as "sound," "good," "weak," or "unsound"; he judged fewer than 3,000 to be sound, and excluded all the others from his compendium. Both al-Bukhari and the editors of other collections of hadiths that appeared in the ninth century were learned and painstaking scholars. Yet they have been widely criticized during the last hundred years for assigning undue importance to the credentials of the chain of authorities transmitting a particular hadith and paying too little heed to the intrinsic merits or plausibility of the text itself. In any case, it is often argued, the so-called science of verifying hadiths was useful chiefly for making the study of genealogy and historical biography such a prominent feature in Islamic life; sifting the evidence more than two hundred years after the event was bound to be so faulty that all hadiths might as well be considered apocryphal. The judgment of an Indian Muslim, writing in the late nineteenth century, is typical:

[6] Adapted with modified spelling and punctuation from Arthur Jeffrey, ed., *Reader on Islam* (Mouton, 1962), p. 86.

The vast flood of traditions soon formed a chaotic sea. Truth and error, fact and fable mingled together in an undistinguishable confusion. Every religious, social, and political system was defended, when necessary, to please a Khalif or an Ameer to serve his purpose, by an appeal to some oral traditions. The name of Mohammad was abused to support all manner of lies and absurdities, or to satisfy the passion, caprice, or arbitrary will of the despots, leaving out of consideration the creation of any standards of test. . . . I am seldom inclined to quote traditions having little or no belief in their genuineness, as generally they are unauthentic, unsupported, and one-sided.[7]

A generation later, a British scholar made a more generous evaluation:

But however sceptical we are with regard to the ultimate historical value of the traditions, it is hard to overrate their importance in the formation of the life of the Islamic races throughout the centuries. If we cannot accept them at their face value, they are of inestimable value as a mirror of the events which preceded the consolidation of Islam into a system. Many of the political, dynastic, religious, and social differences which agitated Islam in the days of its imperial might are illustrated in traditions promulgated by the conflicting parties in the interest of their pretensions. In them we see how the rival forces of militarism and pacifism, asceticism and materialism, mysticism and literalism, free will and determination, strove fiercely for the mastery.[8]

Even a spurious hadith may reveal an issue that aroused feelings strong enough for men to put words in the mouth of the Prophet. And traditions such as the one quoted above, with its report of the Prophet's gentle treatment of

[7] Moulavi Cheragh Ali, *The Proposed Political Reforms in the Ottoman Empire and Other Mohammadan States* (Bombay, 1883), pp. xix and 147, as quoted by Alfred Guillaume, *The Traditions of Islam* (Oxford University Press, 1924), p. 29.

[8] Guillaume, *The Traditions of Islam*, pp. 12–13.

the man who broke the ban on sexual activity during the daylight hours of Ramadan, endow the austere figure of Muhammad with warmth and humor.

The Last Judgment

There is little that is gentle or humorous, however, in the urgent warnings relayed by Muhammad in the early revelations of the Koran. Everyone must realize, he insists, especially the stubborn materialists and polytheists of Mecca, that the Last Judgment is no remote contingency but something that may have to be faced a few moments after death. The very titles of some suras are arresting: "The Terror" (56), "The Mustering" (59), "The Darkening" (81), "The Splitting" (82), "The Earthquake" (99), "The Clatterer" (101). The verses themselves convey the awfulness of the Last Day:

> When heaven is split open,
> when the stars are scattered,
> when the seas swarm over,
> when the tombs are overthrown,
> then a soul shall knows its works, the former and the latter.

. . . .

> When the sun shall be darkened,
> when the stars shall be thrown down,
> when the mountains shall be set moving,
> when the pregnant camels shall be neglected,
> when the savage beasts shall be mustered,
> when the seas shall be set boiling,
> when the souls shall be coupled,
> when the buried infant shall be asked for what sin she was slain,
> when the scrolls shall be unrolled,
> when heaven shall be stripped off,
> when Hell shall be set blazing,
> when Paradise shall be brought nigh,
> then shall a soul know what it has produced.[9]

[9] Arberry, *The Koran Interpreted, II*, Suras 82 and 81, 328 and 326.

Souls will be consigned to eternal punishment or reward:

> Faces on that day humbled,
> labouring, toilworn,
> roasting at a scorching fire,
> watered at a boiling fountain,
> no food for them but cactus thorn
> unfattening, unappeasing hunger.
>
> Faces on that day jocund,
> with their striving well-pleased,
> in a sublime Garden,
> hearing there no babble;
> therein a running fountain,
> therein uplifted couches
> and goblets set forth
> and cushions arrayed
> and carpets outspread.[10]

Many Westerners have expressed shock not so much at the gruesome punishments of the Muslim hell as at the sensual delights of the Islamic paradise with its "maidens good and comely, houris, cloistered in cool pavilions, untouched before them by any man or jinn" and its promise of indulgence in unique beverages ("no brows throbbing, no intoxication").[11] Yet, "the highest joys even there are spiritual," as Carlyle observed, and they may be summed up in the word *salaam,* "peace." *Salaam alaykum* ("peace be upon you, peace be with you") is the universal greeting among Muslims. Verse after verse in the Koran insists that the peace of paradise is reserved for those who have faith and who fear the Lord. The damned are the unbelievers, those who deny the Last Judgment or commit the unforgivable sin of suggesting that God could have partners.

---

[10] Arberry, *The Koran Interpreted,* II, Sura 88, 336.
[11] Adapted from Arberry, *The Koran Interpreted,* II, Suras 55 and 56, 253 and 254.

Man and God

The Koran demanded that Muslims affirm the unity of God and warned Christians to abandon the doctrine of the Trinity because it violated the strict canon of monotheism: "People of the Book, go not beyond the bounds in your religion, and say not as to God but the Truth. The Messiah, Jesus son of Mary, was only the Messenger of God, and His Word that He committed to Mary, and a Spirit from Him. So believe in God and His Messengers, and say not, 'Three.' "[12]

The Prophet, although entrusted with God's message, never claimed to have the power that lies at the heart of the Christian view of Jesus—that of interceding with God on behalf of man. Allah is, in effect, unapproachable and incomprehensible. This concept of the deity goes far to account for the reputation of Muslims as fatalists, accepting with equal composure good fortune or ill because both represent "the will of Allah."

But Islam is a religion of hope as well as of resignation. According to a hadith, Muhammad stated that God had 99 "most beautiful" names in addition to Allah and would admit to paradise any Muslims who had committed them all to memory. Aiding memorization is the "Islamic rosary," the "worry beads" that Muslims so often finger, which consist of a string of 99 beads, or one of 33 beads to be negotiated three times. The 99 names, drawn partly from the Koran and partly from the hadiths, stress both the stern and the gentle aspects of Allah. Here are the Koranic verses containing the 13 names heading the list:

> He is the All-merciful, the All-compassionate.
> He is the King, the All-holy, the All-peacable.
> the All-faithful, the All-preserver,

[12] Arberry, *The Koran Interpreted*, I, Sura 4, 125.

> the All-mighty, the All-compeller,
> the All-sublime.
> He is God,
> the Creator, the Maker, the Shaper.
> To Him belong the names Most Beautiful.[13]

The first two names are found in the *bismillah* or *basmala*, the invocation that prefaces every sura of the Koran except one and that Muslims very frequently employ as a blessing —*bismillah ar-rahman ar-rahim* ("in the name of Allah, the merciful, the compassionate").

A popular literature has grown up to illustrate the attributes associated with the 99 names. A typical one shows God's capacity to observe everything everywhere and to show compassion toward the mightiest and the lowliest of his creatures, as he commands the angel Gabriel:

> Go earthward! pass where Solomon hath made
> His pleasure-house, and sitteth there arrayed,
> Goodly and splendid—whom I crowned the king—
> For at this hour My servant doth a thing
> Unfitting: out of Nisibis there came
> A thousand steeds with nostrils all a-flame
> And limbs of swiftness, prizes of the fight;
> Lo! these are led, for Solomon's delight,
> Before the palace, where he gazeth now
> Filling his heart with pride at that brave show;
> So taken with the snorting and the tramp
> Of his war-horses, that Our silver lamp
> Of eve is swung in vain, Our warning Sun
> Will sink before his sunset-prayer's begun;
> So shall the people say, 'This king, our lord,
> Loves more the long-maned trophies of his sword
> Than the remembrance of his God?' Go in!
> Save thou My faithful servant from such sin.

[13] Abridged from Sura 59. Arberry, *The Koran Interpreted*, II, 270. The complete list of the 99 may be found in *The Encyclopaedia of Islam*, new ed., s.v. al-Asma' al-Husna, and in Edwin Arnold's *Pearls of the Faith*.

> Also, upon the slope of Arafat;
> Beneath a lote-tree which is fallen flat,
> Toileth a yellow ant who carrieth home
> Food for her nest, but so far hath she come
> Her worn feet fail, and she will perish, caught
> In the falling rain; but thou, make the way naught,
> And help her to her people in the cleft
> Of the black rock.[14]

Many Muslim personal names are derived from the 99—Abd-ar-Rahman ("slave of the merciful one"), Abd-al-Karim ("slave of the generous one"), Abd-al-Wahhab ("slave of the giver")—not to mention Abd Allah or Abdullah. The recurring *Abd* invokes again the central Islamic doctrine of submission by reminding us that a Muslim is quite literally one who can say, in the words of the Koran, "I have surrendered my will to God."[15]

---

[14] Arnold, *Pearls of the Faith* (Boston: Roberts Bros., 1883), pp. 6–8.
[15] Arberry, *The Koran Interpreted*, I. Sura 3, 75.

THE PILLARS
OF THE FAITH

The Muslim's surrender to God imposes on him certain obligations, the most binding of which are called the five Pillars of the Faith. The five are as follows: subscribing to the confession of faith, performing the ritual prayers, giving alms, observing the fast of Ramadan, and making the pilgrimage to Mecca. Although there are many other elements of belief and practice that set Islam apart from other great religions, the five Pillars remain the most distinctive.

Confession of Faith

According to the *Shahada*, or confession of faith, the Muslim must testify: "there is no God except Allah, and Muhammad is the apostle of God." Although this celebrated formula is based on a hadith, its two clauses may be found in separate suras of the Koran, and its spirit is wholly Koranic. The Muslim confession of faith is sometimes described as essentially negative, just as Islam itself is characterized as essentially passive. Yet in Muhammad's day it was a positive and dangerous step to reject the Meccan polytheistic tradition and accept the validity of Muhammad's prophetic mission. It is also worth reiterating that the Koran presents Muhammad as "naught but a Messenger" and also asserts that "The Messiah, son of

Mary, was only a Messenger."[1] However, while Muhammad rejected both for himself and for other prophets
the superhuman qualities attributed to great religious
leaders, a certain aura of infallibility soon came to surround
the figure of Muhammad. In the Islamic tradition he is
less than a Messiah but he is more than a Prophet.

Prayers

The requirements for worship constantly remind
Muslims that the demands of religion take precedence over
everything else. The times for the five daily prayers are
derived from the Koran as interpreted and supplemented
by the hadiths. Coming at daybreak, at noon, in the middle
or latter part of the afternoon, just after sunset, and before
retiring for the night, they oblige the devout to suspend
activities such as sleep or business or pleasure and put
the everyday world to one side just when it may be most
engrossing. The signal for prayer is given when the *muezzin*
("the caller to prayer") chants his summons from the
minaret. The chant begins and closes with repeated as-
sertions that "God is most great" *(Allahu akbar);* it also
incorporates the Shahada and admonitions to come to
prayer and to good or to salvation, adding, at dawn, that
"prayer is better than sleep."

To prepare for worship the Muslim must do two
things—put himself in the proper state of mind and spirit
to pray and perform his ablutions in accordance with the
command of the Koran: "O believers, when you stand up
to pray wash your faces, and your hands up to the elbows,
and wipe your heads, and your feet up to the ankles."[2]

Water is the favored agent for purification, running
water not still, flowing from a tap or fountain or poured

[1] Arberry, *The Koran Interpreted,* I, Suras 3 and 5, 91, 140.
[2] Arberry, *The Koran Interpreted,* I, Sura 5, 128.

from a receptacle; if there is no water to be had, then the Koran directs the Muslim to "have recourse to wholesome dust."[3] The cleanliness of the worshippers during prayer is protected by the requirement that shoes or boots be left outside the mosque and by the custom of standing and kneeling on a rug or mat during prayer.

The worshiper faces toward Mecca, the direction of which is indicated by a special niche in the Mosque, the *mihrab*. He follows a set sequence of movements and postures: standing, bending from the hips, prostrating himself by touching the forehead, toes, hands, and knees to the ground, then sitting back on his haunches, and finally another prostration and standing. The sequence is traversed a total of two, three, or four times, depending on the hour of the day. At each stage the worshiper recites what is, in effect, a segment of the Islamic creed—the Shahada, or *Allahu akbar*, or the brief opening sura of the Koran, the *fatihah*, which runs as follows:

Praise belongs to God, the Lord of all Being,
   the All-merciful, the All-compassionate,
     the Master of the Day of Doom.

Thee only we serve; to Thee alone we pray for succour.
   Guide us in the straight path,
   the path of those whom Thou hast blessed,
   not of those against whom Thou art wrathful,
     nor of those who are astray.[4]

Both the recitations and the movements and postures are essential to the ritual, for they are the inward and outward tokens of the Muslim's submission. The Arabic word for mosque *(masjid)* means "place of prostration," and it has been suggested that early Muslims stressed prostration and

[3] *Ibid.*, p. 129.
[4] Arberry, *The Koran Interpreted*, I, 29.

other physical exercises as means of disciplining unruly converts.

Muhammad urged Muslims to pray communally whenever possible, notably at noon on Friday, "the day of congregation." Recent scholarship argues that he selected Friday not to be deliberately different from Judaism or Christianity but because it was the day of the weekly market at Medina, and that he chose the hour of noon, despite its heat, because by then the local farmers had largely finished at the market and would soon be ready to return home.[5] At Friday noontime an *imam* ("leader") conducts the faithful in prayer, and a *sheik* ("elder") delivers a sermon, which usually follows a set pattern.[6] It might be supposed that the imam and the sheik are in effect Muslim priests or ministers; actually they are laymen, not necessarily occupying positions of prominence but generally respected for their moral or intellectual qualities. Islam in fact has no priesthood, no agents to whom God has entrusted the power of the keys to the kingdom of heaven, as the Christian God entrusted them to the Catholic priest. Yet we shall encounter many other Muslims in addition to the imam and the sheik who perform a kind of clerical function.

Although many Muslim states observe Friday as the weekly holiday, Muhammad himself seems to have regarded the Friday congregational prayer as an interlude in a normal working day. Moreover, congregational worship is not mandatory in Islam, even on Fridays and even though some Muslims perform nearly all their prayers in the mosque; the prayer rug is always an individual's own private mosque. What is mandatory is that the Muslim

[5] S. D. Goitein, *Studies in Islamic History and Institutions* (Brill, 1966), pp. 111–125.
[6] An example may be found in Kenneth Cragg's, *The Call of the Minaret* (New York: Oxford University Press, 1956), pp. 127–130.

honor the spirit as well as the letter of the law by performing the ritual as a truly humble supplicant. In addition to
the five daily periods of worship, other prayers are recommended, especially at times of danger or of sorrow, such
as a journey or a bereavement. On these occasions certain
popular formulas of prayer are generally followed.[7]

Alms

The third Pillar of the Faith—the giving of alms—
rests on the repeated warnings of the Koran that the
possession of personal property can be justified only if the
owner gives it away freely and generously. Here is a
sample passage:

> Be kind to parents, and the near kinsman,
> and to orphans, and to the needy,
> and to the neighbour who is of kin,
> and to the neighbour who is a stranger,
> and to the companion at your side,
> and to the traveller, and to that your
> right hands own. Surely God loves not
>   the proud and boastful
> such as are niggardly, and bid other men
> to be niggardly, and themselves conceal
> the bounty that God has given them.[8]

In effect, ownership of wealth is not absolute; it is a trust
from God, to be used for God's purposes.

To promote such uses, the Prophet during his years
at Medina separated alms into two categories, the voluntary and the mandatory. The latter involved the payment
of a fraction of a man's income—often fixed at one-fortieth
—to support the Muslim community; this payment was

[7] Examples may be found in Jeffrey's *Reader on Islam*, pp.
522–529.
[8] Arberry, *The Koran Interpreted*, I, Sura 4, 106. "That your
right hands own" refers to slaves.

tantamount to a tithe or poor tax, though still in principle a free-will offering. The tradition of voluntary alms-giving accounts for the widespread toleration of begging in the Muslim world; indeed, an American woman who married a Persian reports that her in-laws, like other well-to-do families, maintained a "house" beggar to whom they gave a regular dole.[9] The tradition also accounts for the frequency with which individual Muslims have assigned real estate or other wealth to a pious foundation (*waqf*) for the endowment of a religious school, a hospital, or some other charitable institution. Down almost to our own day the Muslim world has tended to rely much more on such gifts by individuals than on government or community action to finance social services and welfare.

Ramadan

The fast of Ramadan, the fourth Pillar of the Faith, follows in part pre-Islamic Arab customs, in part ascetic Christian observances such as Lent, and in part the Jewish precedent of fasting on and before Yom Kippur, the solemn Day of Atonement, which occurred when Muhammad arrived in Medina. Muhammad is reported to have selected Ramadan because it was the month of his initial revelation "wherein the Koran was sent down to be a guidance to the people."[10] Ramadan may also have been a traditional Arab holy season; and it may have been chosen, too, in thanksgiving for the victory of Badr, which was won in that month.

The fast itself is very rigorous and demanding, especially when the Islamic lunar calendar brings Ramadan into the heat of summer. Between sunrise and sunset nothing is to enter the body: no food is to be swallowed, nor

[9] Anne S. Mehdevi, *Persia Revisited* (Knopf, 1964), pp. 170–174.
[10] Arberry, *The Koran Interpreted*, I, Sura 2, 52.

any water or other fluid, not even one's saliva; sexual activity is banned, as is smoking; and the faithful should
spend as much time as possible in prayer, preferably at
the mosque. At night, however, customary life may be
resumed "until the white thread shows clearly to you from
the black thread at the dawn."[11] A large meal is consumed
in the evening, and a special one an hour or so before
daybreak. The nights of Ramadan are characterized by
much the same family closeness that Westerners associate
with the Christmas season; reunions and visits are common,
and children are given presents. At sunset, when the last
day of Ramadan has been reached, the skies are searched
for the new moon, and as soon as its sighting has been
verified, preparations begin for the joyous feast, sometimes called the sugar festival of *Bairam*, which breaks the
fast.

Traditionally, only the sick, the aged, travelers,
pregnant women, and nursing mothers are permitted to
defer observing Ramadan until circumstances permit them
to fast. Nowadays, strict observance of Ramadan not only
imposes hardships on the individual but disrupts economic
and administrative routines because working staffs become sleepy, irritable, and inefficient. Yet even in advanced
Muslim countries such as Tunisia and Egypt, proposals to
modify or abandon the fast as incompatible with the demands of modern life have aroused strong opposition. It
has been estimated that the number of Muslims fulfilling
the obligations of the fast exceeds those who perform the
five daily prayers. Why Ramadan continues to be widely
observed is suggested in a letter written by an Iraqi leader
to his son from a prison cell after the Baghdad revolution
of 1958:

It is a spiritual exercise in obedience to Allah
and in appreciation of his blessings. It is a social exercise

11 *Ibid.*, p. 53.

of feeling with the poor and needy and of feeling the
interrelation, unity and equality among all Moslems. It
is a moral exercise, strengthening the will of man and
inculcating in him self-control. It is a physical exercise,
habituating man to bear hunger and thirst.[12]

The Hajj

Ramadan is the ninth month of the Islamic calendar;
the twelfth and final month is also sacred, for it is the
season of the pilgrimage to Mecca, the *hajj*, the fifth Pillar
of the Faith. The Koran urges every Muslim, man or
woman, whose health and circumstances permit, to make
the hajj at least once. As the pilgrim approaches the holy
city, he makes careful preparations to purify himself. Until
completing the hajj several days later, a man shaves his
head, leaving it bare, and puts aside his usual clothing to
wear two plain sheetlike garments in recognition of the
equality of all men before Allah; women, too, wear special
robes. Each pilgrim is required to abstain from sexual
relations and to go without bathing or cutting the hair or
nails during the hajj, so that his physical person will in no
way be diminished while he is concentrating on his religious duties.

When the pilgrim reaches Mecca, he repeats the
actions reportedly performed by Muhammad himself on his
final pilgrimage in A.D. 632. He enters the courtyard of the
Great Mosque in which he finds the ancient Kaaba, covered
with a drapery of black brocade (the drapery is renewed
annually as a gift of the Egyptian government, and remnants of the discarded drapery are sold to the devout). The
pilgrim makes seven circuits around the Kaaba, kissing
the sacred black stone in its wall if the crush of people
permits him to get close enough, or else at least touching

---

[12] Mohammed Fadhel Jamali, *Letters on Islam* (London:
Oxford University Press, 1965), pp. 42–43.

it with his hand. He touches his breast against the adjoining area of wall, believed to be especially sacred, and then drinks from the well of Zamzam near the Kaaba. Next he shuttles rapidly between two small hills just outside the Great Mosque in imitation of Hagar, the discarded concubine of Abraham (see p. 16), whom Muslim tradition describes as running desperately between them seeking water for Ishmael.

On the eighth day of the month of pilgrimage, the faithful journey to the plain of Arafat, a dozen miles east of Mecca, where tradition asserts that Adam and Eve were reunited after their long separation following the expulsion from Eden. Here, on the ninth day of the month, occurs the solemn ritual of the standing at the place where Abraham is believed to have stood against pagan idolatry. From noon until sunset the vast throng of pilgrims stand before the little mountain of Arafat, often called the Mount of Mercy, praying, meditating, and examining their consciences, while sermons are delivered recalling that the Prophet preached at the same place in A.D. 632. Ahmad Kamal, a modern Muslim writer, has described very eloquently what the standing means to the sensitive Muslim:

> *This is the Hajj.* These are the supreme hours.
> The soul-shaken pilgrim entering the Sanctuary of Makkah and for the first time beholding the Holy Ka'bah and the Black Stone knows a humility and an exaltation which are but a prologue for 'Arafat. Here, by the mountain, the pilgrim will pass what should be, spiritually and intellectually, the noblest hours of life. The tents of the Faithful will cover the undulating valley as far as the eye can see. This immense congregation with the sacred mountain at its center is the heart of Islam. This is the day of true brotherhood, the day when God is revealed to His servants.
> We are promised that in these hours by 'Arafat, God will send down His forgiveness and mercy to those who are deserving and they will feel His presence.

> This is the day of brotherhood and heartbreak—
> heartbreak that we have not yet learned to cling to this
> solidarity where we dwell and labor in valleys and
> mountains far from 'Arafat.
>
> This is the day of promise: the guarantee of what
> Islam shall be when Muslims everywhere achieve the
> oneness today known only at 'Arafat.[13]

Something of the oneness experienced at Arafat can
be shared by the whole Islamic community through participation in the Feast of Sacrifice, the *great* festival of the
Muslim Year (the *little* festival marks the end of Ramadan).
On the tenth day of the pilgrimage month, the day after
the standing, Muslims everywhere commemorate the joyful
sacrifice of Abraham when, following the intervention of
the angel Gabriel, he learned that God would accept the
offering of a lamb as a substitute for the sacrifice of his
son. In the Book of Genesis this incident takes place in
Palestine, and Abraham's son is Isaac; in Muslim tradition
the locale is Mina, a suffocatingly hot valley midway between Arafat and Mecca, and Abraham's son is sometimes
identified still as Isaac but more often as Ishmael.

On this tenth day Muslims who are not on the hajj
celebrate with congregational prayer and feasting, following the custom set by Muhammad during his first years at
Medina, when the hostility of the Meccans made it im-
possible for him to visit their city at the pilgrimage season.
The pilgrims themselves gather at Mina, and each one
slaughters a lamb, a goat, or, if he is wealthy, a camel.
He also throws stones at each of three rock pillars symbol-
izing Satan, at whom Ishmael (or Isaac) hurled stones in
terror on three occasions when he expected to be sacrificed.
After the tenth day the pilgrims relinquish their state of
consecration and prepare to resume their usual life. They
are expected to remain at Mina for two or three more nights

[13] Ahmad Kamal, *The Sacred Journey* (Allen & Unwin, 1964),
p. 69.

before making a final circuit of the Kaaba and departing for their homes, often by way of Medina.

The Islamic hajj, like great pilgrimages in other faiths, is an extraordinary medley of the spiritual and the crude, of deeply felt ritual and the distractions of a fair or carnival. It contains many echoes of pre-Islamic beliefs and practices associated with the story of Abraham or, according to some scholars, with an even older pagan cult of exorcising the sun demon to bring an end to the heat and drought of the long desert summer. Traditionally, pilgrims have been importuned and often exploited by guides, peddlers, and adventurers; their health has been threatened by appallingly unsanitary conditions, notably in connection with the massive slaughter of sacrificial animals at Mina on the tenth day. In recent years, vigorous police and sanitary measures by the Saudi Arabian authorities have greatly diminished the hazards and improprieties affecting the hajj, though the combination of brutal heat and vast, excited crowds still poses a peril.

Improvements have also eased the journey to the Hejaz, which was for many centuries both arduous and costly, the pilgrim caravans from Egypt and Syria requiring at least a month for a one-way trip. The completion of the Suez Canal (1869) allowed the establishment of steamer service from the Mediterranean to Jidda, the port of Mecca; a new overland route opened with the completion of the Hejaz Railway from Damascus to Medina in 1908 but was cut when segments of track were destroyed during World War I (reconstruction began only in the mid-1960s). Finally, special air services for pilgrims, inaugurated after World War II, attracted a very wide patronage.

Estimates of the number of pilgrims in a given year were until recently very rough; one study for the third quarter of the nineteenth century put the number at 50,000 for the lowest year and at 150,000 for the highest. The totals appear to have increased erratically thereafter, largely because of the frequent political upheavals in the Middle East. Recently, Saudi Arabian authorities have kept a careful count; during the pilgrimage season of 1967 (which preceded the six-day war between Israelis and Arabs) they reported that well over 300,000 made the hajj—a number estimated to be less than one-tenth of 1 percent of the total Muslim population of the world.

In matters such as these, percentages, totals, and other quantitative measures are inadequate. What really counts is the qualitative factor, and all the evidence suggests that for the average pilgrim the hajj is an overwhelming and unforgettable experience, the greatest of his life. On his return home he is called *hajji* and enjoys a special respect in his community; he also has a feeling akin to that which Christians describe as being saved. The response of a sensitive and articulate pilgrim to the standing at Arafat has already been cited. Even the least sensitive pilgrim apparently has some feeling of awe before God and of brotherhood with his fellow Muslims.

Probably more than any of the other Pillars of the Faith the hajj convinces Muslims of the enormous range, power, and potential of the House of Islam as compared to the House of Unbelief. A modern Western scholar, Bernard Lewis, assesses the hajj as perhaps the most important factor in accounting for the unity in the civilization of medieval Islamic cities "in values, standards and social customs—that is without parallel in the mediaeval west."[14] A modern Muslim political leader, Gamal Abdel Nasser of Egypt, expressed the hopes he cherished when he visited Mecca in 1953 on the occasion of the death of ibn-Saud, the founder of the modern Saudi Arabian kingdom:

> Our idea of the pilgrimage should change. . . . The pilgrimage should be a great political power . . . a regular political congress wherein the leaders of Muslim states,

[14] *The Encyclopedia of Islam*, new ed., s. v. Hadjdj.

their public men, their pioneers in every field of knowledge, their writers, their leading industrialists, merchants and youth draw up in this universal Islamic Parliament the main lines of policy for their countries and their co-operation together until they meet again.[15]

[15] Gamal Abdel Nasser, *The Philosophy of the Revolution* (Economica Books, 1959), p. 77.

THE LAW AND
THE STATE

The Sharia

The five Pillars of the Faith are central supports of the structure of Islamic law. *Structure*, however, is a rather misleading term to use in characterizing the law, for, as an authority on the subject has observed, "The sacred law of Islam is an all-embracing body of religious duties rather than a legal system proper; it comprises on an equal footing ordinances regarding cult and ritual, as well as political and (in the narrow sense) legal rules."[1]

Significantly, Muslims term their law the *Sharia*, which means road or avenue, the way to truth and to Allah. The Sharia is at once more comprehensive than a law code in the Western sense and less tightly organized. Divinely inspired, the Sharia has been revealed to man through the Koran and through the actions and statements of Muhammad recorded in the hadiths; as the handiwork of God, the Sharia is in theory perfect in itself, requiring neither changes nor supplements.

Practice, however, has been another matter, and modern Islamic scholars tend to agree that the Sharia should not be viewed as an immutable set of laws, fixed for

---

[1] J. Schacht, *The Origins of Muhammadan Jurisprudence* (Clarendon, 1950), p. v.

eternity by the Prophet. Whereas the Koran and the hadiths sometimes prescribe proper behavior in great detail, at other times they state ethical principles in very general terms lacking the clear and meticulous qualities the lawyer would expect. As a result, in the first centuries of Islam, ambiguities had to be explained, conflicts resolved, vagueness clarified, and lines drawn between ideal programs and practicalities of the moment. A famous instance is provided by the verses in Sura 4 of the Koran concerning plural marriage and the guardianship of orphans (orphans here in the sense of children whose fathers have died):

> Give the orphans their property, and do not exchange the corrupt for the good; and devour not their property; surely that is a great crime.

> If you fear that you will not act justly towards the orphans, marry such women as seem good to you, two, three, four; but if you fear you will not be equitable, then only one.[2]

These verses seem to have referred to the urgent problem facing the struggling Muslim community in its first years at Medina. Many Muslim men had been slain in the campaigns against the Meccans, leaving widows and orphans to be cared for; plural marriages by the surviving men were an obvious solution. But recommendations for a particular emergency required considerable elaboration to serve as the basis of permanent family legislation.

The Ulema

The task of interpreting the legacy of the Prophet and building the Sharia was accomplished during the first

[2] Arberry, *The Koran Interpreted,* I, 100.

three Islamic centuries (the seventh, eighth, and ninth of
the Christian era). Contributions came from many sources
—from the customs and precedents of the Arabs, termed
the *Sunna,* which also included the life and example of the
Prophet, and from the Jewish, Christian, Byzantine, and
Persian institutions encountered by the rapidly expanding
Muslim community. Although modern scholars do not
agree on the relative weight of each contribution, it is
generally accepted that a role of crucial importance was
taken by Muslim theologians and legal experts. These men
were known collectively as the *ulema,* that is, "those learned
in religion." Although the ulema were laymen and did not
claim priestly powers or authority, they occupied in the
medieval Muslim world a position comparable to that of
the clergy in Christendom, constituting the first estate of
society, commanding great respect, and exerting a very
broad influence. From the ranks of the ulema came both
the *qadis* ("judges") and the scholarly advisers of the *qadis,*
the *muftis,* or jurisconsults, who issued definitive opinions
on the law called *fetwas.*

The ulema nurtured the growth of the law in several
ways. They devised tests of the validity of hadiths—or at
least of the reliability of the chain of transmitters. The
ulema worked out a system of reasoning by analogy from
the precepts of the Koran and the hadiths to suggest how
these sources would have treated topics that they did not
in fact cover adequately, thereby filling gaps in the law.
And they made the consensus of their own views the binding determinant of what was and what was not part of the
law. This supremacy of consensus amounted to an assertion
of the ulema's infallibility in determining important matters
of faith and doctrine. When, about A.D. 900, the ulema
reached the consensus that no further major interpretations
were required, the Sharia was in effect complete. The law
had become set and would remain so for nearly a thousand
years.

The Four Pathways

Yet even then the Sharia was not totally rigid and inflexible, for muftis might always accommodate older interpretations to new or altered situations. Moreover, among the ulema, many different schools of interpretation emerged, varying "pathways to truth," as they were called. Although agreed on many essentials, the different pathways ranged in outlook from the mildly liberal to the sternly fundamentalist. Four of them survived at the close of the Middle Ages and still exist today, each named for its scholarly founder. They are listed below in order of increasing conservatism.

(1) The *Hanafi* is the most flexible, famous for the maxim that "The legal rule is not unchangeable. . . . It expresses what generally happens and changes with the circumstances which have produced it."[3] Based at first in Iraq, it became established in the Ottoman Empire after the Turkish conquest of the Middle East and is today the official school in most of the Middle Eastern states (except for the Arabian peninsula) and in Afghanistan, Pakistan, and the Muslim communities of India.

(2) The *Maliki*, the oldest of the four, grew out of the legal practices of Medina, the Muslim capital during Muhammad's last ten years and for a quarter century after his death. The founder was a judge and the compiler of the first treatise on the Sharia. Today the Maliki prevails in the Muslim areas of North and West Africa.

(3) The *Shafii* was founded by a most influential jurist, who flourished about A.D. 800 and placed much greater stress on the guidance of hadiths than on that of legal precedents or circumstances. The Shafii was the official school of the Abbasid caliphate at Baghdad (to be discussed later in this chapter), and it prevails today in northern Egypt and in the Muslim communities of East Africa, Southeast Asia, and Indonesia.

[3] Quoted by D. de Santillana in "The Law and Society," *The Legacy of Islam* (London: Oxford University Press, 1931), p. 305.

(4) The *Hanbali*, which reacted strongly against what it considered the innovations of the other three, sought to return to the uncorrupted Islam of Muhammad's day. (Its founder is said to have refused watermelon because he had no testimony that the Prophet had ever eaten it!) The Hanbali stronghold is among the Muslim fundamentalists of Saudi Arabia.

Despite the differences among the four, each of them has long accepted the other three as orthodox. In many Muslim countries a person may be judged, if he requests, according to the interpretations of a school different from the one officially recognized in the particular state. This latitude is particularly significant in Israel, Jordan, Lebanon, and Syria, where the Hanafi school of the old Ottoman Empire still has official status; but a majority of Muslims now favor other pathways. The relatively peaceful coexistence of divergent pathways is a striking instance of the Muslims' capacity for mutual toleration.

Human Conduct and Human Rights

From its very beginnings the Sharia was greatly concerned with the conduct of the individual Muslim. Among the requirements it imposed—and still enforces, with varying degrees of severity—were the circumcision of boys and the observance of certain taboos. The Sharia forbade gambling and the consumption of alcoholic beverages (an extension of the Koranic ban on wine). It banned the eating of pork but generally followed the Koran in rejecting other Jewish dietary restrictions because they were, in Muslim eyes, punishments visited by God upon the Jews for their disobedience. Reflecting Muhammad's hostility to the high interest exacted by moneylenders in Mecca and among the Jews of Medina, the Sharia forbade usury, which it defined very broadly to include most forms of interest and profit as they are understood in the West.

Later, the ulema developed the principle that an investor could be justified in receiving a return on his capital only if he participated in an enterprise in a direct personal fashion. Various legal strategems or fictions were devised to enable a man to meet the requirements of the law and still make a profit. The jurists of the Hanafi school were particularly helpful in developing a code of commercial law that reflected the very large role taken by Muslim merchants in Mediterranean trade during the Middle Ages.

The Sharia regulated the formation and operation of the charitable *waqf* endowments and also the allocation of estates to the relatives of the deceased. It generally directed that, in matters of inheritance, the woman's proper portion should be half that of a man. On the whole, the Sharia acknowledged that women had some rights, though they were markedly inferior to those of men. Whereas there were few grounds on which a wife could divorce her husband, all the man had to do was repudiate his wife and pass a three-month waiting period, to ascertain that she was not pregnant, before the divorce became final. Although a woman might not have more than one husband, the Koran permitted a man four wives provided that he treated them all with equal generosity. Polygamy has usually been more the exception than the rule in Islamic society, if only because relatively few men have been able to afford more than one wife. When a Muslim takes a second wife today, he does so most often because the first has not borne him a son. Instances of Muslim leaders taking wives beyond the Koranic maximum often represent political marriages, entered into to insure the loyalty of restless tribes or factions. Such was the case with Muhammad himself, who eventually took nine wives after the death of Khadija, and in the first half of our own century with ibn-Saud, most of whose many wives were hostages for the good behavior of the tribes from which they came. Incidentally, Saudi Arabia continued to apply the harsh punishments sanc-

tioned by the Sharia in its early days—the stoning to death
of a woman taken in adultery, the amputation of a thief's
hand or foot—long after other Muslim states had mitigated
them.

The Sharia accepted the existence of slavery, though
it recognized that slaves had certain rights, such as that to
own property. There are many examples in Islamic history
of men who were technically slaves and yet achieved great
wealth and power. Although many slaves were Blacks from
Africa, the basic inequalities among men recognized in
Islamic law and custom arose not from race or skin color
but from religion. It was the duty of Muslims to convert
pagans and polytheists to Islam or else to exterminate them
in the holy wars. Jews and Christians, because they were
People of the Book and had received part of God's revelation, could practice their religion with comparative free-
dom; nevertheless, they were treated as inferiors. They
paid heavier taxes, they were barred from such honorable
pursuits as serving in the army or riding horses (the donkey
was their mount), and Christian men were forbidden to
marry Muslim women. Muslim tolerance was far from
absolute, though there is a kernel of truth in the often-
repeated claim that until relatively recent times Muslims
were more tolerant than Christians.

Preoccupied with moral, social, and religious issues,
the Sharia had little to say about politics and public affairs.
Muslim governments had to improvise regulations and
courts to deal with essential administrative matters. This
supplementary legal apparatus came to be called *qanun*,
from the Greek word *canon*, so that canon law, which is
ecclesiastical in the Western world, is wholly secular in
the Islamic tradition. The most urgent political problem
faced by the young Islamic commonwealth was the succession to the leadership of the *umma* when Muhammad
died; this problem was met by the institution of the
caliphate.

The Caliphate

Because Muhammad made no provision for the succession, the stricken Muslim community turned back to tribal precedents of electing a new sheik as soon as the Prophet died. When it seemed likely that this procedure would result in the choice of an unworthy man, three trusted lieutenants of Muhammad intervened to secure the election of one of their number. He was abu-Bakr, one of the earliest converts to Islam and the father of Aisha, the favorite wife of Muhammad in his later years. He took the title Khalifa Rasul Allah—*successor* (or *deputy*) *of the messenger of God*—and the office of caliph came into being.

At first the nature of the caliphate was more political than religious, and it was only when the caliphs had lost most of their actual power many years later that a sacred aura came to surround the caliphate. The early caliphs were in a sense first among equals. Abu-Bakr and his successors were involved chiefly with political and military problems and worked closely with other leaders of the *umma*. In styling themselves deputies of the Prophet, they laid no claim to Muhammad's prophetic gifts but served as imam leading prayers at the Prophet's Mosque in Medina, much as any respected layman might in his local mosque.

It has sometimes been argued in the West that the caliph is the Muslim counterpart of the pope; the contention, however, has little validity. There is no separation of church and state in Islam, as there is in much of Christendom. Indeed, there is no Muslim Church as such—no formal hierarchy, no priesthood, but only lay leaders, the caliph in practical affairs, and the ulema in theological and intellectual matters.

Muslims call the age of the first four caliphs, A.D. 632 to A.D. 661, that of the Rashidun, the righteous or orthodox rulers (Rashid is one of the 99 names of God). But it was also a period of mounting strife within the *umma*, marked by the violent deaths of all three followers of abu-Bakr. Tension heightened under the fourth caliph, Ali (A.D. 656–661), the son of Muhammad's uncle-protector, abu-Talib, and the husband of Muhammad's daughter, Fatima. Ali had expected that his double kinship to the Prophet plus his reputation as a very early and pious convert to Islam would insure his selection as caliph much sooner. His long-standing sense of grievance was little soothed by his belated arrival at the caliphate, for it aroused much opposition among both the wealthy Meccans, who had been in the ascendancy under the third caliph, and the inner circle of Muslims at Medina. Ali therefore removed his capital from Medina and the Hejaz to Kufa in Iraq; but he was never able to subdue a chronic rebellion by the governor of Syria, Muawiya, a member of the powerful Umayyad family of Mecca. When Ali was slain by a religious zealot in A.D. 661, the caliphate passed to Muawiya and was to remain in Umayyad hands for almost a century, down to A.D. 750. The capital, transferred from Kufa to Damascus in Syria, was never to return to Arabia.

A Century of Expansion

Even more significant for the future of Islam than the upheavals in the caliphate was the breathtaking series of conquests begun by the Rashidun caliphs and completed by the Umayyads. Within ten years of Muhammad's death Syria, Iraq, and Egypt had all come under Muslim control, and with such ease that their trade and agriculture suffered little disruption. In the east the Muslims later took over the crumbling Sasanid Empire in Persia and extended their frontiers to the fringes of India and China. To the west the Muslims pushed across the lands of the Berbers, a non-Semitic people for whom the Barbary coast

of North Africa, from the western boundary of Egypt to
the Atlantic, is named. In A.D. 711 the Muslims crossed from
Morocco to Spain and conquered the rickety Visigothic
kingdom established on the debris of the Roman province
of Hispania. The commander of the expedition, the Berber
Tariq, gave his name to the great rock on the European
side of the strait that lies between Morocco and Spain—
Jebel Tariq ("Tariq's mountain") or Gibraltar—and the invaders gave theirs to a whole epoch in Spanish culture,
called Moorish because they had crossed from Mauretania,
the former Roman province in northwestern Africa. The
high-water marks of the Islamic tide in Europe were the
long but unsuccessful Arab siege of Byzantium (A.D. 717–
718) and the Battle of Poitiers in A.D. 732, when the Franks
defeated a force from Moorish Spain that had penetrated
deep into western France. In the ninth century Muslims
from North Africa conquered the nearby Mediterranean
island of Sicily, which they held for more than two centuries
until their expulsion by the Christian Normans.

What were the motives behind Muslim expansion
and the reasons for its astonishing rapidity and success?
Until a century ago the West assumed that the fanatical
spirit of jihad drove invincible armies half way around the
world. In the late nineteenth century the focus shifted
from religion to economics and geography, and particularly
to the hypothesis that the Arabs, no longer able to sustain
themselves in a country that was becoming progressively
more arid, exploded out of "the hot prison of the desert."
Present-day experts view this hypothesis with much cau-
tion, since the most recent archaeological evidence suggests that no marked change for the worse had occurred
in the climate of Arabia for at least several centuries before
Muhammad's day. Today the search for explanations turns
to the catalytic impact of a dynamic religion on the restless and disorganized Arabs. Bernard Lewis has given a
persuasive evaluation of the effect of Islam:

> Its importance lies in the temporary psychological change which is wrought in a people who were naturally excitable and temperamental, unaccustomed to any sort of discipline, willing to be persuaded, but never to be commanded. It made them for a time more self-confident and more amenable to control. In the Wars of Conquest it was the symbol of Arab unity and victory.[4]

Muhammad himself appears to have decided in his last years that armed expansion would best serve to counter potential enemies abroad and to channel the aggressive energies of Arabs at home. Hence the large expedition organized in A.D. 630 to penetrate along the road to Syria. As soon as the Prophet died, many Arab tribes considered their allegiance to have lapsed, since they had given it to the person of Muhammad as a kind of supersheik rather than to the community of Islam. Abu-Bakr and his generals dealt with the crisis by extending Muhammad's expansionist policy. Placing Bedouin warriors of uncertain loyalty under reliable Meccan commanders, they waged war simultaneously against both Arab apostates and the Byzantine and Persian empires. The exhaustion of both empires after a generation of mutual conflict emboldened the Arabs. They encountered little resistance from the decaying Sasanid regime in the great river valleys of Iraq, though the difficult mountain terrain farther east slowed their advance through Persia. Though the rugged mountains of Anatolia and the Balkans prevented the conquest of the Byzantine heartland, the Arabs plucked off the Byzantine provinces of Syria and Egypt, which, as we have already seen, were disaffected from their old rulers on religious and political grounds.

In all this, as G. E. Von Grunebaum has observed with pardonable exaggeration, "no one gave a thought to

[4] Bernard Lewis, *The Arabs in History* (Torchbooks, 1960), p. 56.

the conversion of non-Arabs."[5] The principal architects of Arab success were quite secular men, with no great personal religious commitment. Their basic strategy was to strike at the Fertile Crescent by exploiting their "desert power," which Lewis likens to modern seapower:

> The desert was familiar and accessible to the Arabs and not to their enemies. They could use it as a means of communication for supplies and reinforcements, as a safe retreat in times of emergency. It is no accident that in each of the conquered provinces the Arabs established their main bases in towns on the edge of the desert, . . . using existing cities like Damascus when they were suitably placed, creating new ones like Kufa and Basra in Iraq, Fustat in Egypt, Quirawan in Tunisia, when necessary. These garrison towns were the Gibraltars and Singapores of the early Arab Empire. In them the Arabs built their cantonments and garrison cities and throughout the Umayyad period they remained the main centres of Arab government.[6]

The Umayyads, A.D. 661-750

The Umayyad caliphs did not abandon all their desert ways when they moved the capital to the ancient city of Damascus. They built a series of palaces in the Syrian desert or on its fringes (the ruins of several of them may still be found in Jordan); and they continued to rule, like Arab sheiks of old, with the help of tribal dignitaries. This was rule by a conquering minority, an aristocracy of Muslim Arab warriors exploiting a majority that was at first neither Muslim nor Arab.

The subsequent interaction of rulers and ruled greatly changed the status of both. The caliphs brought

---

[5] G. E. von Grunebaum, *Classical Islam* (Aldine, 1970), p. 53.

[6] Lewis, *The Arabs in History*, p. 55.

from Arabia few of the institutions required for governing a large empire that was the heir of many ancient cultures. They therefore borrowed at first not only the administrative organs, personnel, and procedures of the preceding regimes but also their language and coins. In Iraq and Iran, the government of the caliphate acquired a Persian flavor, and in Syria and Egypt a Byzantine one. Islamic architecture acquired a splendor appropriate for an imperial regime, as the Umayyad caliphs sponsored the construction of the magnificent Dome of the Rock in Jerusalem and the Great Mosque in Damascus. The tides of influence also flowed in reverse. In the eastern Muslim domains the Arabic language vied with Persian, which adopted the Arabic alphabet and added many Arabic words to its vocabulary, while retaining its Indo-European grammar. In Syria Arabic largely supplanted Aramaic, and in Egypt it eclipsed the non-Semitic Coptic tongue.

At the same time that the Islamic domains were undergoing this linguistic Arabization, the Arab character of Islam itself was being diluted, as the faith gained millions of converts among Persians, Syrians, Copts, Berbers, and other non-Arab peoples. The converts, many of whom were prosperous merchants and craftsmen in the expanding garrison cities, felt that they deserved social and political status commensurate with their economic success. Though the Umayyads did eventually grant them the same tax exemptions enjoyed by Arab Muslims, the concession was too little and too late to offset the resentment of the new Muslims at the exclusiveness of the dominant Arab minority. A second source of unrest was the growing contingent of people who believed that the caliphate should have passed to Ali's descendants and regarded Muawiya and the other Umayyads as usurpers; these were the Shiites, from the Arabic *Shiat Ali* ("party of Ali"). Still other difficulties never surmounted by the Umayyads were the chronic feuds between Arabs who came originally from the northern regions of the peninsula and those from the southern, and the alienation felt by Iraqis and Persians, who were long accustomed to being at the center of a great empire and aggrieved to be subordinated to a government at Damascus.

The Abbasids, A.D. 750-1258

Under the last Umayyad caliphs almost everyone with a grievance seemed to rally to the family of the Abbasids, named for their ancestor al-Abbas, a brother of Ali's father and an uncle of Muhammad. Promising to purify Islam, to make additional concessions to the converts, and to restrict the power of the Arab aristocracy, the Abbasids raised the standard of revolt and in A.D. 750 swept the Umayyad caliph out of office. The event has been called "a turning point in the history of the Muslim state," "as important . . . as the French and Russian revolutions in the history of the West."[7] It marked a social revolution by the underprivileged non-Arab Muslims; it prompted a long series of bids for religious revolution by Muslim reformers and dissidents, as the next chapter will show; and it produced revolutionary changes in the nature of the caliphate.

The Abbasid caliphs moved from Damascus to the new city of Baghdad on the Tigris in Iraq, close to the old Sasanian capital of Ctesiphon. They acted less like the heirs of Arab sheiks and warriors and more like the successors of the emperors who had ruled over Mesopotamia hundreds and thousands of years before. The caliphs claimed to be monarchs by divine right, calling themselves "God's shadow" and asserting virtually unlimited authority. They maintained their court with the ceremony and glamor of

[7] The first quotation is the title of an essay by S. D. Goitein, in *Studies in Islamic History and Institutions* (Brill, 1966); the second is from Lewis, *The Arabs in History*, p. 80.

The Arabian Nights and were open-handed patrons of learning and the arts, especially generous to non-Arab Muslims and to converts from Christianity and Judaism. They were cosmopolitan, too, in choosing official personnel: for ministers and bureaucrats they favored Persians, and for soldiers Turks, impressive fighters from Turkestan in the steppes of Central Asia, who were beginning to filter westward and accept Islam. Many of these Turks were Mameluks, that is, the slaves of the caliph; however, this servile legal status did not prevent many Mameluks from rising to posts of great influence.

Turkish soldiers and Persian officials took over most of the actual authority from the caliph, leaving him as a remote figurehead. The seeds of political deterioration were planted very early in the five centuries of history of the Abbasid caliphate, as early as the reign of the celebrated Harun ar-Rashid (A.D. 786–809), the contemporary of the Western ruler Charlemagne. In Iraq and Persia the alliance of dissidents and malcontents who had brought the Abbasids to power broke into troublesome factions, as so often happens with revolutionary coalitions. The more distant provinces of the Empire were already proclaiming their independence or autonomy, first Spain (A.D. 756) under a refugee Umayyad emir (or *amir*—the Arabic word means *commander* and, by extension, *prince*) with his capital at Cordova. By the close of the eighth century the Spanish example had been followed by Morocco and Tunisia, with their independent Berber populations. Later Egypt, Syria, Persia, and the Arabian peninsula all slipped away from the control of Baghdad, so that the effective authority of the Abbasids was confined largely to Iraq. The fiction of formal Islamic unity under a single caliph ended in the tenth century when the Umayyad Emir Abd-ar-Rahman III proclaimed himself caliph in Spain and the Shiite Fatimids (named for Fatima, the daughter of Muhammad and wife of Ali) followed suit in North Africa. In the year 1000 there were three caliphs—in Baghdad, in Cordova, and in Cairo.

External pressures also weakened the Abbasid caliphate, as new Asian invaders violated its eastern frontiers. In the eleventh century the most formidable group of Turks yet to appear overran Persia and captured Baghdad; these were the Seljuks (named for an early leader). The Seljuk chieftain won from the caliph recognition as *sultan*, which means *the man with authority*, particularly over political and military affairs. The Seljuk sultans, now the real rulers of the caliphate, briefly revitalized Islamic power, conquering most of Anatolia from the Byzantines in the 1070s and setting in motion the chain of events that led the alarmed Byzantine emperor to appeal to the pope and culminated in the Crusades.

By the time the first crusading force arrived from the West, the Seljuk sultanate was already breaking into fragments—a fact that goes far to explain the initial successes of the Crusaders. They took Jerusalem in 1099 and made it the capital of a feudal kingdom. But the Crusaders' power was confined largely to cities and castles on the eastern shore of the Mediterranean and its immediate hinterland; Muslims retained control of key inland cities like Aleppo and Damascus, lying on the inner rim of the Fertile Crescent facing the desert. Credit for delivering the Crusaders a mortal wound by recapturing Jerusalem in 1187 went to Saladin, who was neither Turkish nor Arab but Kurdish. (The Kurds are a mountain people still living in the Tigris watershed in eastern Turkey and northern Iraq and Iran; they claim descent from the Medes of antiquity and speak a language related to Persian.) Saladin, whose gallantry won him the reputation in the West of being the "Robert E. Lee" of the Crusades, cast a long shadow over the future of the Abbasid caliphate by establishing a new dynasty of sultans with their capital at Cairo and their power base in Syria as well as in Egypt.

The End of the Caliphate

Thus, when the Mongols captured Baghdad in 1258, they did not destroy a flourishing regime, as Westerners have often supposed; the Abbasid caliphate had passed its prime long before. After 1258 there were still Abbasid caliphs, at least in name, maintained at Cairo for purposes of prestige by the Mameluk sultans who had seized control of Egypt and Syria from the successors of Saladin. For all practical purposes, however, the office of caliph had ceased to exist. Saladin had already ended the Fatimid caliphate in North Africa; and the Umayyad caliphate in Cordova had collapsed even earlier under the triple blow of internal factionalism, new Berber invasions from Africa, and the pressure of Christian Crusaders from northern Spain. Berber dynasties reinvigorated Moorish Spain for a time; but in the thirteenth century the Christians resumed their reconquest, which Ferdinand and Isabella brought to completion in 1492 by capturing the last Moorish stronghold at Granada.

At the close of the Middle Ages the major center of Muslim power was the Empire of the Ottoman Turks or Osmanli, who took their name from an early chieftain, Osman. Beginning as petty local rulers in the no-man's-land along the Seljuk-Byzantine frontier in northwestern Anatolia, they gradually conquered a vast empire. At the peak of their success, under Suleiman the Magnificent (1520–1566), their domains included most of Hungary and Southeastern Europe as well as North Africa and the Middle East. The capital of the Ottoman Empire was Byzantium, renamed Istanbul after the Turks captured it in 1453, and the titles borne by their emperor included that of caliph, transferred from the Abbasid puppet in Cairo. The Ottoman emperors seldom used the title and showed little interest in the potentialities of the caliphate until the late nineteenth century, when Abdul Hamid II launched a

Pan-Islamic policy to court the support of Muslims everywhere and bolster his tottering regime against the inroads of European imperialism. One fruit of his policy was the construction of the Hejaz Railway to carry pilgrims from Damascus to Medina.

Defeat in World War I overwhelmed the Ottoman Empire and led to partition of its territories, with the Turkish-populated core in Anatolia established as a republic. In 1924 the Turkish republic formally abolished the caliphate; though many Muslims regretted its disappearance, efforts to revive it under Indian or Arab auspices were soon abandoned. In fact, the caliphate had lost its raison d'être a thousand years before at the beginning of the Abbasid era, when it became evident that one man could not hope to rule the vast Islamic domains stretching from the Atlantic to the steppes east of the Caspian Sea.

In 1924, also, the Turkish republic abandoned the Sharia, regarded as the legacy of an outworn past. This action aroused not only regrets but also strong opposition from many Muslims, both inside and outside Turkey, because it seemed to strike at the vitals of Islam in a way that the demise of the caliphate did not. In the Ottoman Empire the leading legal expert, the grand mufti, ranked second only to the emperor and bore the proud title, *Sheikh ul-Islam* ("the Elder of Islam"). In the twentieth century the Sharia still retained some of its raison d'être, even though its literal application would cripple the building of the progressive secular society envisaged by the founders of the Turkish republic and other modern-minded Muslim leaders. Today few Muslim countries except Saudi Arabia attempt to apply the Sharia in totality, but few have followed Turkey's precedent in endeavoring to discard it altogether. In the Islamic world the law has proved to be more enduring than the state.

ORTHODOXY AND HETERODOXY

A major cause of the distorted images of Islam in the West has been the mistaken assumption that all Muslims share identical beliefs and follow similar practices. With its four legal pathways and its three rival medieval caliphates, Islam, too, proved to be a house with many mansions. The Muslims, like the Christians, have their puritans, their fundamentalists and modernists, and their mystics and hysterical devotees. As in most of the world's great religions, there is a norm in Islam, a central position of orthodoxy occupied by the average Muslim. The majority consider themselves to be Sunni Muslims, but there is a large minority of Shiites and other nonaverage Muslims.

Sunnis and Dissidents

Historically, the Sunnis are the faithful observers of the Sunna of the Muslim community, that is, the customs based on the Koran, the hadiths, and the precedents followed by the Prophet and the Rashidun caliphs. The Sunni, in their own eyes, have been the only orthodox Muslims; and their interpretations of the Sunna, their policies and behavior in general have formed the mainstream of the Islamic tradition. All four legal pathways, for example, are Sunni.

Although Islamic orthodoxy was able to accommodate a considerable range of differences, disagreements arose almost at the beginning of Muslim history that were too profound to be accommodated within the Sunni community. And so heretical or heterodox sects emerged to denounce the powers that were and to bear witness to the intertwining of political, religious, and socioeconomic strands in Islamic history. Lewis has stated the matter very instructively:

> Whenever a grievance or a conflict of interests created a faction in Islam, its doctrines were a theology, its instrument a sect, its agent a missionary, its leader usually a Messiah or his representative. But to describe these socially motivated religious heresies as "cloaks" or "masks", behind which scheming men hid real and material purposes . . . is to distort history. The Islamic State, born of Muhammad's community in Medina and fostered by the ancient divine monarchies of the Orient, was in theory and in the popular conception a theocracy, in which God was the sole source of both power and law and the sovereign His viceregent on earth. The faith was the official credo of the established order, the cult the external and visible symbol of its identity and cohesion, conformity to them, however perfunctory, the token and pledge of loyalty. Orthodoxy meant the acceptance of the existing order, heresy or apostasy its criticism or rejection.[1]

The Kharijites

The earliest of the dissident sects, the *Kharijites* ("seceders") appeared a quarter of a century after Muhammad's death, during the caliphate of Ali. In dealing with Muawiya, the rebellious Umayyad governor of Syria, Ali accepted an offer of arbitration rather than joining battle and was outwitted as a result. Thereupon several thousand of his supporters mutinied, claiming that only Allah can arbitrate, whereas men are obliged to fight. As a leading

[1] Lewis, *The Arabs in History*, p. 99.

Kharijite spokesman later put it, "It is not the tongue, but the actions of your hands that appease the heart."[2] The Kharijites were militant puritans and activists, who took the law into their own hands. They made jihad the sixth Pillar of the Faith and were so convinced of their own righteousness that they felt justified in killing any Muslim whose conduct was less ascetic than their own. Ali himself, deemed unworthy to be caliph, was the victim of a Kharijite assassin in A.D. 661.

The Kharijites also condemned the practice of having only men from the Meccan tribe of Quraish serve as caliph; the caliphate should be open to all Muslims, even to black slaves. Their egalitarian fervor and their hostility to the Arab aristocracy won them many adherents among the Bedouin Arabs and the non-Arab converts to Islam. While the Kharijites were a thorn in the flesh of the early Umayyad caliphs, later the anarchist tendencies implicit in their distrust of all established authority divided the Kharijites into ineffectual and antagonistic factions. Kharijite communities survive today in scattered areas of the Muslim world—in some Berber districts of Algeria and Tunisia, in the East African state of Tanzania, and in Oman, the remote land at the eastern tip of the Arabian peninsula. The fiercely puritanical Kharijite spirit has inspired the zealotry of some later Muslim reformers, notably the Wahhabis of Saudi Arabia.

Shiism

Shia Islam, which originated as a movement to restore the caliphate to the family of Ali, soon assumed a remarkable and distinctive religious coloration. Although scholars have not yet been able to reconstruct all the de-

---

[2] Quoted by Elie Adib Salem, "Political Theory and Institutions of the Khawarij," *The Johns Hopkins University Studies in Historical and Political Science*, LXXIV (1956), 495.

tails of its metamorphosis, one major element in it was the Shiite conviction that the Umayyad and Abbasid caliphs set out systematically to eradicate the descendants of Ali. Shiites believe that Muawiya, Ali's successor as caliph, poisoned Hasan, the elder son of Ali and Fatima; Sunnis, on the contrary, contend that Hasan died peacefully. Then, when Hasan's younger brother, Hussein, rebelled in A.D. 680, he was slain at Karbala, near Kufa in Iraq, under atrocious circumstances: badly wounded, tormented by thirst, he was tortured by the "Sunni dogs," who denied him water until at last they cut off his head. The anniversary of Hussein's death—the tenth day of Muharram, which is the first month of the Islamic year—is the major Shia religious holiday, observed with more intensity than the great feast commemorating the sacrifice during the month of pilgrimage, or the little feast terminating Ramadan. Shiite tradition further asserts that Hussein's son was later poisoned, as was his grandson—and so on for several generations.

The essential quality of Shiism resides in its transformation of these victims of political maneuvering into semidivine martyrs. The transformation apparently occurred under the influence of the gnostic and dualistic teachings of other religious traditions in the Fertile Crescent and Persia. Gnostic comes from the Greek word *gnosis*, which means *knowledge of God* and was used in Greek translations of the Old Testament; gnosticism referred to the processes, often partaking of a kind of magic, which enabled the initiate to know God, to move from the visible world to an invisible and higher realm beyond. The Neoplatonists, who flourished in Alexandria in the second and third centuries A.D., converted Plato's philosophy of idealism into a gnostic cult. Gnosticism also promised men the ability to penetrate beyond the literal meaning of a great prophetic text such as the Bible or the Koran and grasp its secret inner meaning.

A certain dualism was evident in all the monotheistic religions, especially in Christianity with the contrast between the perfection of the heavenly city and the corruption of man's earthly city. The idea of two great sets of forces contending for the soul of man was carried to an extreme in two of the religions prevalent in Sasanid Persia —Zoroastrianism and Manicheism, each named after its first prophet. Both interpreted the universe in terms of a polarity between opposite elements—good and evil, light and dark, fire and earth. The Manicheans, whose ideas later inspired the famous medieval Christian heresy of the Albigensians, were profoundly pessimistic, because they felt that the forces of Satan were so strong that few men had the fortitude and virtue to win through to the good.

By incorporating so many beliefs from religions other than Islam, Shiism became a syncretistic faith, assimilating its borrowings into a new synthesis, in which the central figures were Ali, Hasan, Hussein, and their descendants. They were called imams, but imams in a much more exalted sense than the Sunni leader of congregational prayer. A nineteenth-century Shia theologian summarized their attributes:

> It is necessary to believe that Imams were created from one pre-existing Light; that all blessings and all knowledge of God come through them; that through them the universe lives and moves and has its being; and that they are in every respect the most excellent of beings after the Prophet Muhammad, and superior to all other Prophets and to the Angels, though subject to all human needs and functions. They are also immaculate, innocent of any sin, small or great, co-equal, endowed with every virtue, knowledge and power. Their birth was not as that of ordinary mortals, and, like the Prophet, they were born circumcised.[3]

[3] E. G. Browne, A History of Persian Literature in Modern Times, A.D. 1500–1924 (Cambridge University Press, 1924), pp. 394–395.

The imam could reveal to the faithful the esoteric inner meaning of the Koran and lead them from darkness into light, from corruption into blessedness. The magical infallibility attributed to the imams by the Shiites greatly exceeded any powers claimed by the Sunnis for their caliphs; the Shiites introduced into Islam the concept of a mediator or intercessor between man and God which seems more compatible with the Christian view of Jesus than with the austere monotheism of Muhammad.

The focal point of the Shiite religious year is the first ten days of the month of Muharram, which constitute a period of mourning and special devotions, when the faithful repeat the lament, "*Ya Hasan, ya Hussein,*" groaning and weeping and sometimes beating themselves with chains. On the tenth day itself they may attend a passion play, reenacting with great realism the suffering of Hussein. The audience has on occasion become so overwrought that actors portraying the Sunni persecutors have been assaulted. It is as if the tragedy of Karbala had occurred only yesterday, not almost thirteen hundred years ago.

The intense emotionalism of the Shiites and their ingrained suspiciousness and intolerance rank high among the factors separating them from the Sunni Muslims. Von Grunebaum has observed that "the nervous climate of the Shi'a is still that of a suppressed sect, even where not only political recognition but political sovereignty has been achieved."[4] A still more decisive element of separateness is the Shia concentration on Ali and the succeeding imams to the virtual exclusion of Muhammad. Shiites are less concerned with Mecca and Medina than with pilgrimages to their own holy places, notably the tombs of the imams themselves or of their relatives or protectors. A special sacredness surrounds the tomb of Hussein at Karbala, where so many Shiites have been buried that it has long been celebrated as a city of the dead.

[4] Von Grunebaum, *Muhammadan Festivals*, p. 85.

To the outsider, Shia Islam seems a gloomy faith, obsessed with death, martyrdom, and grief. Yet it is by no means without its promise of hope, contained in the concepts of the hidden imam and the Mahdi. Most Shiites recognize the existence of twelve imams, beginning with Ali, then Hasan, then Hussein, and so on until the twelfth, a young lad who disappeared at Samarra in Iraq in the year A.D. 873. The twelfth imam vanished but he did not die; rather, as the hidden imam, he entered a prolonged "concealment" from which he would one day emerge as the "expected one," the Mahdi, the new Messiah. A medieval Shiite creed characterizes the Mahdi in these words:

> He it is concerning whose name and descent the Prophet was informed by God, and he it is who WILL FILL THE EARTH WITH JUSTICE AND EQUITY JUST AS IT IS NOW FULL OF OPPRESSION AND WRONG. He it is whom God will make victorious over the whole world until from every place the call to prayer is heard and religion will belong entirely to God, exalted be He. He is the rightly guided *Mahdi* about whom the prophet gave information that when he appears, Jesus, son of Mary, will descend upon the earth and pray behind him.[5]

Understandably, the later history of Shia Islam records many figures who claimed to be the hidden imam rejoining mankind as the Mahdi.

Twelvers and Zaidis

The *Twelvers*, as the main body of Shiites is rather awkwardly termed, form a significant minority in the Muslim world today. In Iran, where Twelver Shiism has been the state religion since the sixteenth century, they

    [5] Quoted by J. A. Williams, ed., *Islam* (Braziller, 1961), pp. 228–229.

constitute the overwhelming majority. In Iraq the Shiite community nearly equals the Sunni in size but has traditionally been much inferior to it in social and political influence, and very much affected by the "nervous climate" noted by von Grunebaum. In Lebanon, an area which has long been a haven for persecuted sects, the Shiites make up about 18 percent of the population and are generally considered to be the most impoverished major religious grouping in the country. In Pakistan and India the Shiites constitute about one-twelfth of the total Muslim population. In Morocco the ruling dynasty has been Shiite since the end of the eighth century, though the prevailing legal code is Maliki, one of the four Sunni pathways.

Not all Shiites are Twelvers. The Zaidis recognize only the first four of the usual imams, ending with the son of Hussein. They take their name from Hussein's grandson, Zaid, who, like his grandfather, was slain leading a rebellion in Iraq. In practice, there is little to distinguish the Zaidis from the Sunni except for their refusal to recognize the legitimacy of the caliphs following Ali. Although they insisted that their imam should be a descendant of Hasan or Hussein, they did not make any extraordinary claims for his infallibility or his mediation between man and god; he was simply a kind of monarch. At the close of the ninth century, the Zaidis won control of Yemen in South Arabia; and, though the majority of the population remained Sunni, Zaidi imams continued to reign for more than a thousand years until the revolution of 1962 made Yemen a republic.

Ismailis and Assassins

At the opposite pole from the Zaidis were the Ismailis or Seveners, the most fascinating and controversial of Muslim sects. Their name originated in their contention that the Twelver Shiites had unjustly accused the seventh imam, Ismail, of drunkenness and recognized his younger brother instead. The Ismailis undertook a vigorous campaign to vindicate Ismail, proclaiming his descendants to be hidden imams. In the process they carried to great lengths the Shiite tendency toward syncretism, particularly in adopting the dualistic practices of gnostic cults. The Ismailis appear to have preached an elementary faith for the literal-minded masses and a much more sophisticated version for the initiate, who could penetrate below the surface meaning of Muhammad's revelations to reach their true inward significance.

In politics the Ismailis disseminated fiery propaganda against the Abbasid caliphate and organized themselves into a revolutionary secret society to achieve its overthrow. For a time they came close to reaching their goal. Toward the end of the ninth century, a hundred years after the death of Ismail, they took advantage of the mounting debility of the Abbasid caliphate and launched a vigorous missionary campaign among discontented peasants and urban workmen, especially in Iraq. Associated with the Ismailis were the militant Carmathians (named after their leader, Qarmat), who ravaged Iraq and Syria, swept across the Arabian peninsula, attacked caravans of pilgrims and, in A.D. 929, even took Mecca. To the horror of the faithful, the Carmathians temporarily carried off the sacred black stone from the Kaaba.

Another group of Ismailis seized power in North Africa by exploiting the chronic tensions between Arabs and Berbers. In A.D. 909 they brought their hidden imam out of concealment and proclaimed him the Mahdi and also the first caliph of the Fatimid line. From their capital in Tunisia the Fatimids soon extended their dominion over the bulk of North Africa and the island of Sicily; in A.D. 969 they conquered Egypt and founded a new city adjacent to the older capital of Fustat, naming it al-Qahira ("the victorious"). Cairo, as we term it, became a busy economic

and intellectual center. There the Fatimid caliphs maintained a great library and built the mosque of al-Azhar
("most shining"), the seat of a celebrated theological university that recently celebrated its thousandth birthday. The Fatimid caliphate reached its peak early in
the eleventh century, when it also ruled Palestine and
Syria and quite overshadowed the decadent Abbasid caliphate in Iraq. By the end of the century, however, internal
weakness and the incursions of new invaders like the Seljuks and the Crusaders had sapped Fatimid strength. Increasingly powerless Fatimid caliphs hung on at Cairo
until 1171, when Saladin took the city, suppressed Ismaili
teachings, and restored the sway of Sunni Islam over
Egypt and Syria.

The Ismailis, however, did not fade out of history
along with the Fatimids. A Persian leader of the sect had
broken with the Cairo caliphate at the end of the eleventh
century and entrenched himself and his followers in a
Persian mountain fortress south of the Caspian Sea. Thus
emerged the Assassins or *hashishin,* who were alleged to
be addicted to hashish because it gave them a foretaste of
paradise and afforded them superhuman courage in com-
bat. Although modern scholarship has found the charge of
drug addiction groundless, the identification of the Assassins with political executions is thoroughly established.
Their assassinations were acts of ritual murder, the weapon
was always a dagger, the assassin himself was almost always caught and did not attempt to escape, and the victim
was a highly placed individual. The first victim was Nizam
al-Mulk, the very capable chief minister of the Seljuk
sultan, Malikshah; among other celebrated victims were
an Abbasid caliph and a Crusader king of Jerusalem. The
Assassins took advantage of the disintegration of the Seljuk
domains in the twelfth century to secure additional strongholds in remote areas of Persia and in the mountains of
western Syria. The Crusaders particularly dreaded the

Syrian Assassins and their chieftain, the sheik al-Jebel ("the Old Man of the Mountain," or less picturesquely, "Lord of the Mountain").

The Assassins' employment of terror as a weapon recalls the tactics of other fanatical minorities. The Assassins' ultimate goal seems to have been the establishment of the reign of their own hidden imam, for which the major prerequisite was the destruction of Sunni Islam. The Assassin chieftain in Persia claimed to be acting on instructions from the hidden imam, who directed him to repudiate the five pillars of the faith and the Sharia in order that all would be in readiness for the reception of a new revelation. The point was underlined at a great ceremony staged during Ramadan in which the worshipers prayed with their backs toward Mecca and partook of an elaborate afternoon banquet.

The Assassins' expectations were never fully realized; Sunni Islam did not crumble, nor did their own hidden imam establish his domain. In the thirteenth century, weakened by internal dissension, the Assassins were subdued in Persia by the Mongol invaders and in Syria by the Mameluks of Egypt, who had succeeded Saladin's dynasty as rulers of the western Fertile Crescent. A remnant of the sect survived, and in the nineteenth and twentieth centuries emerged from obscurity under the leadership of a family of imams who had fled from Persia to India, bearing with them the Persian court title of Agha Khan. The modern followers of the Agha Khan depended on business success, not assassinations, to advance their cause.

Alawis and Druzes

Ismaili missionary activities also fostered the creation of some sects so strongly syncretistic in character and incorporating so many non-Islamic elements that they are often classified as separate faiths. The most prominent examples are the Alawis and the Druzes. The Alawis ("worshippers of Ali") carry to the extreme the Shiite deification of Ali and the Ismaili dichotomy between the simple faith of the many and the more elaborate cult of the initiate. The Alawis also retain features of ancient pagan cults, such as the veneration of groves of sacred trees, follow a ritual adapted largely from Christianity, and celebrate Easter and Christmas. They believe in the transmigration of souls, which must undergo seven incarnations before obtaining release from earthly bondage.

Today, the major center of the Alawis is in the Syrian Arab Republic, where they comprise about 10 percent of the population and live mainly in the Jebel Alawi, the mountainous hinterland of the Syrian coastal region. Manifesting to a high degree the nervousness of a persecuted minority, they gained a reputation for clannishness, discontent, and rebellion. After World War II, however, many young Alawis took advantage of the opportunities for advancement offered by the new liberal enrollment policy at the officers' training academy for the Syrian army. In 1971 one of these officers, General Hafiz al-Assad, became the first Alawi, and the first non-Sunni, to hold the Presidency of the Syrian Republic. Alawi beliefs also influenced the clandestine heterodox Turkish sects known as Kizilbashi ("redheads," from the distinctive headgear they wore).

The Druzes trace their origins and their name to an eleventh-century Ismaili missionary, Darazi, whose followers proclaimed the Fatimid Caliph Hakim to be the hidden imam. Hakim, a very eccentric ruler, vanished one evening near Cairo in the year 1021 and, in the judgment of non-Druzes, was probably murdered. Seeking to practice their faith unmolested and to live undisturbed according to a strict feudal pattern, the Druzes found a refuge in the mountains of southern Lebanon and, later, also in the highlands of southern Syria, the Jebel Druze. They long made a fetish of secrecy, concealing their sacred books even from most members of the sect and refusing to accept new converts or to permit apostasy from their ranks. To avoid persecution, the Druzes practiced dissimulation, denying their own faith and professing that of their overlords, usually Sunni Muslims or Lebanese Christians. The outside world first gained some knowledge of their beliefs in the 1830s, when control over Syria and Lebanon passed for a few years from the Ottoman Empire to the Egyptians, who permitted Western scholars to study the Druze sacred books.

The Druzes pride themselves on being unitarians, regarding Caliph Hakim as a manifestation of the Cosmic One, evidently a kind of incarnation of God. To the outsider, in any case, they appear to claim an identity between their hidden imam and God more complete than that claimed for Ismail by the Ismailis or for Ali by the Shiites. The details of Druze doctrine and practice show many radical departures from Muslim norms. Among the Druzes polygamy is forbidden, women are treated with a large measure of equality, and belief in the transmigration of souls is widespread. The Druzes do not observe Ramadan or make the hajj, though they do celebrate the great feast of the pilgrimage season. They hold their weekly congregational services on Thursday evenings, not Friday noon, and at remote mountain shrines rather than at centrally situated mosques. The Druze community is divided into "the ignorant," who are allowed to attend only the less secret parts of the weekly service, and "the sages," who wear distinctive white turbans and are expected to lead austere and exemplary lives. Whereas any Druze, no matter how lowly in origin, may become a sage, a few great landowning families have long monopolized social and political leadership. The feudal social structure together with the comparative security afforded by a tradition of secrecy and a mountain habitat explains the survival of the Druzes over all these centuries. Today, the Druzes number about a quarter of a million, living chiefly in Lebanon and Syria; some of them live under Israeli rule, in villages near Haifa and also on the Golan Heights, and have the reputation of cooperating more loyally with the government than do the other Arabs under Israeli rule.

Babis and Bahai

The Ismaili doctrine of an esoteric inner life and the Shia belief in a hidden imam have both figured prominently in the genesis of the modern heretical offshoot of Islam, the Bahai faith. In the mid-nineteenth century, a young religious scholar of extraordinary personal charm and persuasive fluency taught in the Persian city of Shiraz. He called himself the *Bab,* a word which means *door* or *gate* in Arabic and, by extension, the *gateway to truth;* the name Bab had been applied to the senior disciple of the Shiite imam a thousand years earlier. In 1844, the thousandth anniversary (by Islamic calculation) of the disappearance of the twelfth imam at Samarra in A.D. 873, the Bab declared himself to be the hidden imam and the Mahdi, and some of his followers began to revere him as an incarnation of God. Babi teachings incorporated many gnostic elements, among them the belief in invisible worlds and in the sacredness of the number *19*—thus the Babi calendar arranged the year into 19 months, each with 19 days. In Persia Babism won so many converts eager to purify the corrupt existing regime that it seemed to threaten the state itself as well as the established religion of Twelver Shiism. The government repressed a Babi rebellion with great severity, executing the Bab (1850) and massacring many thousands of his followers.

Babism did not perish, however, and most of the Babis who survived acknowledged as their leader a disciple of the Bab who styled himself Bahaullah ("the splendor, or glory, of God"). Bahaullah taught that the old cycle of prophets, including Adam, Abraham and other Old Testament leaders, Zoroaster, Jesus, and Muhammad, had come to an end with the Bab. Thus the Bahai, as the followers of Bahaullah styled themselves, contend that their faith alone is truly universal and contains not only all the religions of the old prophetic cycle but also the precepts of Buddha and Confucius, whom Bahaullah regarded with approval. The Bahai retain the Babi calendar, prescribing a congregational assembly every nineteen days, and they observe both a month of fasting, on the model of Ramadan, and a thrice-daily regimen of ablution and prayer, rather similar to that of Muslims, though simpler and briefer.

The most distinguishing feature of Bahaism, besides its broad tolerance, is its strong commitment to social betterment, which is in spirit closer to the Christian tradition than to the Islamic, though it is based on a statement attributed to Ali: "All private matters belong to the human sphere, all concerns of society to the divine." The Bahai include among the "concerns of society" the attainment of equality by women, the promotion of universal education, and the achievement of international peace. By principle, the Bahai are pacifists, conscientious objectors, and teetotalers; by preference, they may also be vegetarians and nonsmokers.

Like the Babis before them the Iranian regime regarded the Bahai as traitors to national unity and subjected them to intermittent persecution. Many Bahai, as a result, practiced dissimulation, and some emigrated; estimates of their number in Iran, which range from less than half a million to a million or more, are at best very approximate. The international headquarters of the Bahai faith is at Haifa in Israel, where the Bab is buried in a splendid tomb on Mount Carmel; nearby, in the vicinity of Acre, Bahaullah lived in exile. Today, there are Bahai communities in 139 countries all over the world. In the United States, where the son of Bahaullah spread the faith, the Bahai have an imposing temple at Wilmette, near Chicago.

The Bahai claim for their faith in the twentieth century what Muhammad claimed for Islam in the seventh —to be the repository of spiritual truth and the successor of all previous religions. Muslims, therefore, regard the Bahai not simply as heretics but as upstart competitors, practitioners of an entirely separate and false religion. Yet the Bahai faith owes a great debt to both the orthodox and the heterodox elements in the Islamic tradition. One such element, which exerted a great influence on the Bab, is the nexus of mystical beliefs and practices known as Sufism. The Sufis, who were even more important in Islamic history than the Shiites, require a chapter to themselves.

SUFISM

The history of religion records many energetic re-
actions against worldly contamination of the faith. In
ancient Judaism the Hasidim ("saints") strove to counter
the Persian and Greek influences widespread in the Fertile
Crescent under the Empire of Alexander the Great; modern
Hasidic communities strive for religious purity by isolating
themselves from the world about them. Catholicism experienced a long cycle of decay and renewal, with each
renovating impulse centered in one of the great religious
orders—the Benedictines of the sixth century, the Cluniacs
of the tenth and eleventh, the Cistercians of the twelfth,
and the Franciscans and Dominicans of the thirteenth.
Almost every period of renovation was followed by new
backsliding, a process that culminated in the secularized
and corrupt Church of the Renaissance and the subsequent
Protestant revolt. In the seventeenth century a new generation of Protestants, among them the English Friends and
the German Pietists, were in turn rebelling against the
formalism of established Protestant churches. Islam, too,
has witnessed a sequence of degeneration, protest, and
purification, associated above all with the mystical doctrines
and institutions known collectively as Sufism.

Sufism Defined

Although attempts have been made to trace the
term *Sufism* to the Greek *sophia* ("wisdom") or to an
Arabic root meaning *purity*, most scholars agree that *Sufi*

comes from the Arabic word for *wool, suf*. Imitating the Christian hermits of Syria, the first Sufis wore coarse woolen garments rather than cotton and reacted to the political and religious dissension of the early Muslim centuries by withdrawing from the world to cultivate asceticism and saintliness. Soon, the Sufis began to stress their absorption with the love of God and with the processes that might lead to direct experience of God. Verses attributed to the eighth-century poetess, Rabia al-Adawiya, proclaimed the Sufi's overwhelming devotion to Allah:

> I love Thee with two loves, love of my happiness,
> And perfect love, to love Thee as is Thy due.
> My selfish love is that I do naught
> But think on Thee, excluding all beside;
> But that purest love, which is Thy due,
> Is that the veils which hide Thee fall, and I gaze on Thee,
> No praise to me in either this or that,
> Nay, Thine the praise for both that love and this.[1]

"That the veils which hide Thee fall, and I gaze on Thee"—this comes about as close as words can to communicating the essentially incommunicable experience of the mystic. Sufis were far less concerned with their fate in eternity than with their yearning to penetrate the veils and achieve gnosis, the knowledge of God. Witness the prayer of the poetess Rabia: "O God, if I worship Thee for fear of Hell, burn me in Hell, and if I worship Thee in hope of Paradise, exclude me from Paradise; but if I worship Thee for Thy own sake, grudge me not Thy everlasting beauty."[2]

Sufism may well appear more compatible with the gnostic faiths of the pre-Islamic Middle East than with the

---

[1] Quoted by H. A. R. Gibb, *Mohammedanism*, 2nd ed. (New York: Oxford University Press, 1953), p. 133.
[2] A. J. Arberry, trans., *Muslim Saints and Mystics* (University of Chicago Press, 1966), p. 51.

teachings of Muhammad, who put so much emphasis on the
Day of Judgment. Yet Sufis justified themselves as good
Muslims by noting that the ninety-nine names of God
stressed his perfection and radiance as well as his sternness
and power. They also cited Koranic verses describing the
closeness of Allah:

> We indeed created man; and We know
> what his soul whispers within him,
> and We are nearer to him than the
>   jugular vein.
>
> .   .   .   .
>
> Hast thou not seen that God knows whatsoever is
> in the heavens, and whatsoever is in the earth?
> Three men conspire not secretly together, but He
> is the fourth of them, neither five men, but He
> is the sixth of them, neither fewer than that,
> neither more, but He is with them, wherever they
> may be.[3]

Sufism and Shiism shared a common hostility toward
the Sunni establishment and a marked disposition toward
syncretism. Yet between Sufi and Shiite there was an important difference, well formulated by a modern authority
on Islamic mysticism: "The Sufis are not a sect, they have
no dogmatic system, the *tariqas* or paths by which they seek
God 'are in number as the souls of men' and vary in-
finitely, though a family likeness may be traced in them
all."[4] This family likeness may be defined as the Sufis'
total commitment to a quest, to a way of life, to what
Sir Hamilton Gibb has called "the organized cultivation of
religious experience."

[3] Arberry, *The Koran Interpreted,* II, Suras 50 and 58, 234,
264.
[4] Reynold A. Nicholson, *The Mystics of Islam* (Routledge &
Kegan Paul, 1963), p. 27.

The Pilgrim's Way

The pathway to God, the *tariqa*, began with the individual's awakening, which the Sufis called *repentance*
for an earlier misdirected life. Subsequent stages along the
pilgrim's way were characterized as abstinence, renuncia-
tion, poverty, patience, trust in God, and acquiescence in
the will of God. The Sufi wayfarer could attain each successive stage by a mounting effort to obliterate self in submission to Allah. Paralleling the stages were spiritual and
emotional conditions—longing, hope, fear, love—over which
the pilgrim had no control, since they emanated directly
from God. Traversing the various stages and conditions of
the *tariqa* prepared the Sufi for reunion with God.

Tales and legends about Sufi heroes clothed these
abstractions with the reality of human experience. The
role they played in medieval Islam correspond to that of
the lives of saints in medieval Christianity: they edified
and inspired the faithful, and they also supplied some
rousing stories. The following episode from the career of
a central Asian king will illustrate this Islamic hagiographi-
cal literature:

> Ebrahim ibn Adham's saintly career began in the
> following manner. He was king of Balkh, and a whole
> world was under his command; forty gold swords and
> forty gold maces were carried before and behind him.
> One night he was asleep on his royal couch. At midnight
> the roof of the apartment vibrated as if someone was
> walking on the roof.
>
> "Who is there?" he shouted.
>
> "A friend," came the reply. "I have lost a camel,
> and am searching for it on this roof."
>
> "Fool, do you look for the camel on the roof?"
> cried Ebrahim.
>
> "Heedless one," answered the voice, "do you seek
> for God in silken clothes, asleep on a golden couch?"
>
> These words filled his heart with terror. A fire

blazed within him, and he could not sleep any more.
. . . Visions by day followed the hearing of voices by
night, equally mysterious and incomprehensible.

"Saddle my horse," Ebrahim cried at last. "I will
go to the hunt. . . ."

. . . Headlong he galloped across the desert; it
was as if he knew not what he was doing. In that state
of bewilderment he became separated from his troops.
On the way he suddenly heard a voice.

"Awake!"

He pretended not to have heard, and rode on.
A second time the voice came, but he heeded it not.
A third time he heard the same, and hurled himself
farther away. Then the voice sounded a fourth time.

"Awake, before you are stricken awake!"

He now lost all self-control. At that instant a deer
started up, and Ebrahim prepared to give chase. The
deer spoke to him.

"I have been sent to hunt you. You cannot catch
me. Was it for this that you were created, or is this what
you were commanded?"

"Ah, what is this that has come upon me?" Ebrahim cried.

And he turned his face from the deer. He thereupon heard the same words issuing from the pommel
of his saddle. Terror and fear possessed him. The revelation became clearer yet, for Almighty God willed to
complete the transaction. A third time the selfsame voice
proceeded from the collar of his cloak. The revelation
was thus consummated, and the heavens were opened
unto him.

Sure faith was now established in him. He dis-
mounted; all his garments, and the horse itself, were
dripping with his tears. He made true and sincere repentance. Turning aside from the road, he saw a shep-
herd. . . . Looking closely, he saw that he was a slave
of his. He bestowed on him his gold-embroidered cloak
and his bejewelled cap, together with the sheep, and
took from him his clothes and hat of felt. These he
donned himself. All the angelic hosts stood gazing on
Ebrahim.

"What a kingdom has come to the son of Adham,"
they cried. "He has cast away the filthy garments of the
world, and has donned the glorious robes of poverty."[5]

Dervish, Sheik, and Brotherhood

Because the Sufi pilgrim usually cultivated poverty
he might be called a *faqir* (from the Arabic word for
poor man) or more commonly a *dervish* (perhaps from a
Persian term for *beggar*). In obedience to the Koranic in-
junction to remember Allah at all times, the dervish repeated the word *Allah* over and over or an affirmation
such as "There is no god but God." This kind of ritual
repetition formed the Sufi litany or *dhikr* (from the Arabic
word for *recollection* or *reminder*). The function of the
litany was described by al-Ghazali, the leading philosopher
of Sufism:

> The window into the unseen is opened in waking
> hours for the gnostic who has striven and is purified,
> being delivered from the power of sensual desire. Such
> a gnostic, sitting in solitude, who closes the channels of
> the senses, and opens the eye and ear of the spirit, and
> places his heart in relation with the Divine World,
> while he says continually: "God, God, God" within his
> heart, not with his tongue, ceases to be aware of him-
> self, and of this world, and remains seeing only Him
> Who is Most Glorious and Exalted. Then that window
> is opened and he sees in his waking moments that which
> he sees in dreams, and there appear unto him angelic
> spirits and the prophets and wondrous forms, fair and
> glorious to behold, and the kingdom of the heavens and
> the earth are laid open unto him and he sees what it is
> not lawful to describe. This gnosis goes far beyond the
> knowledge of the learned, for it enters the hearts of the
> prophets and the saints direct from the Creative Truth

[5] A. J. Arberry, trans., *Muslim Saints and Mystics* (University of
Chicago Press, 1966), pp. 63–65.

Himself, nor can it be comprehended except by those
who have experience of it.[6]

The psychologist might define the dhikr as a technique of
achieving ecstasy through self-hypnosis; the layman might
describe it as a way of "turning on."

Each *tariqa* had its characteristic dhikr, and to
master it the dervish associated himself with a teacher or
director called a sheik or a *pir* (from the Persian word for
saint). Al-Ghazali insisted on the necessity of guidance and
discipline:

> For the way of the Faith is obscure, . . . and he who has
> no shaikh to guide him will be led by the Devil into
> his ways. Wherefore the disciple must cling to his shaikh
> as a blind man on the edge of a river clings to his leader,
> confiding himself to him entirely, opposing him in no
> matter whatsoever, and binding himself to follow him
> absolutely.[7]

The term *tariqa* designated such an association of master
and disciples as well as the Sufi path itself; and this sense
of brotherhood or fraternity respresented the closest Muslim
equivalent to the Christian monastic order. At its core
were the sheik and his dervishes, practicing a strict asceticism so that they might devote themselves exclusively
to the dhikr; supporting them were the lay brethren who
participated in some of the activities of the *tariqa* and
also led normal workaday lives outside it.

Many *tariqas* developed formal structures, with the
sheik assuring continuity by designating his successor, the
khalifa (from the same Arabic root as *caliph*) or, more picturesquely, *the master's prayer rug;* in noncelibate brotherhoods son frequently succeeded father as leader. Two dis-

[6] Margaret Smith, *Readings from the Mystics of Islam*
(Luzac, 1950), pp. 65–66.
[7] Quoted by Gibb, *Mohammedanism,* pp. 150–151.

tinctive types of Sufi brotherhood also emerged. The "urban" orders were marked by moderation and by ties with the ulema of Sunni orthodoxy; the "rustic" orders won a wider popular following and often engaged in practices denounced by the ulema as unorthodox borrowings from paganism or Shiism or Christianity. As we examine a few examples of each type, remember that the history of Islam records nearly two hundred major Sufi orders plus innumerable branches and offshoots, not to mention unaffiliated individual dervishes or faqirs.

The Urban Orders

The largest urban order, the Qadiriya, is named for its twelfth-century founder, Abd-al-Qadir al-Gilani, a teacher identified with the ulema of the fundamentalist school. Like other founders of Sufi orders, al-Gilani came to be regarded as a saint; today his tomb at Baghdad is still under the care of his descendants and continues to attract many pilgrims. The Qadiriya has branches throughout the Muslim world, from North and West Africa to Indonesia, some of them less moderate and peaceable than the parent body. A characteristic dhikr of the Qadiriya is a litany praising Allah, beseeching his pardon, invoking his blessing on Muhammad—each phrase repeated one hundred times—followed by five hundred repetitions of "There is no god but God."

Another universal order is the Naqshbandiya. Its founder urged his disciples to cleanse their hearts by silently drawing pictures on them and was nicknamed Naqshband ("the painter") in consequence. Spreading across Asia from Turkey to China and Malaysia, the Naqshbandi dervishes have played a particularly important role on the Indian subcontinent, where they mitigated some of the chaotic effects of undisciplined sufism and restored Islamic orthodoxy and dignity.

The Naqshbandi consider themselves to be spiritual aristocrats; so too did the adherents of the more localized order, the Mevleviya, who were celebrated for their *dhikr*. It consisted of disciplined dancing or pirouetting, head tilted back, one arm pointing to the heavens, the other to the earth, and accompanied by the gentle music of flute, strings, and drum. The performance lasted for some forty-five minutes, until the participants sank to the floor in exhaustion and ecstasy. In popular tradition these were the "whirling" dervishes, although the label was actually more suitable for the more frenzied movements of a rowdier rustic order. The Mevleviya was an urban order, named for its founder, Mevlana ("our teacher"), the affectionate title bestowed on the Persian poet and mystic, Jalal ad-Din Rumi (1207–1273), who settled at Konya, in central Anatolia, the capital of the Seljuk sultanate of Rum (that is, east Roman or Greek—the reference is to territory that had so long been part of the Byzantine Empire).

Under the Ottoman Empire, which conquered the Seljuk sultanate, the Mevlevi dervishes won a reputation for tolerance, particularly for assisting Armenians and other Christians attacked by Muslim extremists: The government frequently relied on the Mevleviya to counter the reactionary policies of the ulema. Eventually, decay set in, and the newly-created Republic of Turkey suppressed the order in 1925 as part of its secularizing policy. Throngs of reverent visitors, however, still file through the Mevlevi headquarters at Konya, now a museum, and commemorative performances of the dances are held annually.

The Rustic Orders

The oldest rustic order was the Rifaiya, founded, according to tradition, by a nephew of al-Gilani, founder of the Qadiriya. To perform their dhikr the Rifai formed a circle—hands on one another's shoulders, bodies sway-

ing and chanted so energetically that they won the nick-
name of "howling" dervishes. At the climax of the dhikr
they might fall on swords or snakes, walk through fire, or
eat glass—all with impunity. An offshoot of the Rifaiya,
the Sadiya order, practiced a remarkable dhikr that was
described by an English eyewitness in Cairo more than a
century ago:

> A considerable number of the dervishes (I am sure there
> were more than sixty) laid themselves down upon the
> ground, side by side, as close as possible to each other,
> having their backs upwards, their legs extended, and
> their arms placed together beneath their foreheads. They
> incessantly muttered the word "Allah!" Then the Sheikh
> approached: his horse hesitated, for several minutes, to
> tread upon the back of the first of the prostrate men; but
> being pulled, and urged on behind, he at length stepped
> upon him, and then, without apparent fear, ambled,
> with a high pace, over them all, led by two persons,
> who ran over the prostrate men. The spectators im-
> mediatly raised a long cry of "Allah la la la la lah!" Not
> one of the men thus trampled upon by the horse seemed
> to be hurt; but each, the moment that the animal had
> passed over him, jumped up, and followed the Sheikh.
> Each of them received two treads from the horse; one
> from one of his fore-legs, and a second from a hind-leg.
> It is said that these persons, as well as the Sheikh, re-
> peat prayers and invocations on the day preceding this
> performance to enable them to endure, without injury,
> the tread of the horse; and that some not thus prepared
> having ventured to lie down to be ridden over, have, on
> more than one occasion, been either killed or severely
> injured. The performance is considered as a miracle
> effected through supernatural power which has been
> granted to every successive Sheikh of the Sa'idiya.[8]

Another offshoot of the Rifaiya order is the Ahma-

[8] Abridged, with modernized spelling, from E. W. Lane,
Manners and Customs of the Modern Egyptians (Everyman, 1908),
pp. 458–459.

diya, established in thirteenth-century Egypt to rally the country against the crusading expedition of the French king, Saint Louis. Its founder, Ahmad al-Badawi, has been for seven centuries the most popular Muslim saint in Egypt, and pilgrimages are made to his tomb at Tanta in the Delta during the season of the annual Nile flood. Some scholars believe this to be a Muslim adaptation of older cults celebrating the Nile's fertility; the fairs and orgiastic rites accompanying the pilgrimage also date back to pagan antiquity. The saintly practices attributed to al-Badawi himself suggest Christian antecedents—his fasting for forty days corresponds to Lent, and his custom of prolonged gazing at the sun from a rooftop recalls the pillar-dwelling saint, Simeon Stylites.

Christian influence was pronounced in the case of the Bektashi dervishes, who flourished in the Ottoman Empire and were said to have more than seven million members at their peak. The Bektashi replaced some of the external manifestations of Islam with such Christian actions as confessing to the sheik, lighting ceremonial candles, and partaking of a ritual meal of bread, cheese, and wine; they treated women as equals, permitting them to participate in the dhikr unveiled. Because the Bektashi secretly venerated the twelve imams of Shia Islam, their enormous following among the Turkish soldiery made them potential traitors in the frequent campaigns between the Sunni Ottoman Empire and Shiite Persia.

Liabilities and Assets

It is easy to understand why so many of the Sufi brotherhoods have come under Sunni censure for their un-Islamic lapses. In North Africa, especially in Morocco, they intensified the traditional Berber cult of the living saint or holy man called the *marabout* (from an Arabic word meaning *bound* or *tied*) because he was thought to be tied to God. The Sufi sheiks fitted easily into the pattern of the marabouts, whose male descendants were believed to inherit the divine gifts bestowed upon the original saint. On the Indian subcontinent many Sufis adopted Hindu customs still harder to reconcile with Islam, and some faqirs made a profession of exploiting the gullibility of the faithful by taking money in payment for promises of miracles and cures. The following is a critique by Muhammad Iqbal, a leader in modern efforts to reform Islam on the subcontinent:

> Is the organic unity of Islam intact in this land? Religious adventurers set up different sects and fraternities, ever quarreling with one another; and there are castes and sub-castes like the Hindus. Surely we have out-Hindued the Hindu himself; we are suffering from a double caste system—the religious caste system, sectarianism, and the social caste system, which we have either learned or inherited from the Hindus. This is one of the quiet ways in which the conquered nations revenge themselves on their conquerors.[9]

An assessment of the Sufi role in Muslim history, however, will place much more emphasis on its assets than on its liabilities. Although some Sufis degraded Islam, others showed an impressive talent for infusing the faith with new life and endowing it with a broad popular appeal. Sufism figured very prominently in the second wave of Islamic expansion, which began in the eleventh century and achieved results almost as spectacular as those of the great conquests of the first Islamic century. The new wave carried Islam to West Africa, where Berbers overthrew the Black empire of Ghana; to Anatolia, most of which was wrested from Byzantine Christian control for the first time by the Seljuks; and to India, where a dynasty of Turkish

[9] Quoted in Gibb, *Mohammedanism*, pp. 161–162.

slaves, the Ghaznawids, ruled an expanding state in the northwestern part of the subcontinent. Later in the Middle Ages Sufi merchants from India went as traders and missionaries to the Malay peninsula and the Indonesian archipelago. Without the Sufi drive, Islam would probably never have won the converts whose descendants make up the largest Muslim communities in the world today—those of the Indian subcontinent and Indonesia.

Even more important than this external success was the Sufi response to the crises within medieval Islam. At a time when the ulema were concentrating almost entirely on the letter of the law and the quest for orthodoxy, Sufi sheiks, dervishes, poets, and philosophers triumphantly reasserted the supremacy of the spirit. The mystical poetry of the Sufis, their examples of personal devotion and saintliness, and the enthusiasm of their brotherhoods charted new pathways of religious expression just as the older ones were being blocked or narrowed by the ulema. Moreover, Sufism became the involuntary ally of orthodoxy itself when Shiism threatened to eclipse Sunni Islam, in the tenth and eleventh centuries, as the Fatimid caliphate in Cairo overshadowed the declining Abbasid caliphate at Baghdad. Only Sufism could compete with Shiism in emotional fervor and in diversity of appeal. Shiism began to lose ground in the eleventh century and did not begin a partial recovery until the start of the sixteenth century, when the new Safavid dynasty made it the state religion of Persia.

Al-Ghazali

The career and writings of al-Ghazali (1058–1111) furnish the most illuminating example of the contribution made by Sufism to the Islamic tradition. The passages from al-Ghazali quoted earlier in this chapter have only hinted at the revolutionary role played by the man whom Gibb has characterized as standing "on a level with Augustine and Luther in religious insight and intellectual vigor."[10] Like Augustine and Luther, al-Ghazali passed through a major spiritual crisis that had remarkable consequences. Trained by the ulema in theology and the law, he gained youthful fame in Baghdad as a scholar and teacher. Then his encounter with translations of ancient Greek philosophers and with Muslim commentaries on them proved very unsettling. Though he attacked the new emphasis on rationalism in his *The Incoherence of Philosophy*, he also applied Greek logic in his own theological studies. The consequence was a mounting feeling of skepticism about Islam.

As the first step in resolving the crisis, al-Ghazali turned to the writings of the Sufis. "I saw clearly," he later revealed, "that the mystics were men of personal experience not of words, and that I had gone as far as possible by way of study and intellectual application, so that only personal experience and walking in the mystic way were left."[11] The second step was the exceedingly difficult one of acting on these conclusions. Al-Ghazali became convinced

> that the essential thing is to sever the attachment of the heart to this world . . . by rejecting wealth and position and by escaping from entanglements and commitments. . . . I saw I was deeply involved in affairs, and that the best of my activities, my teaching, was concerned with branches of knowledge which were unimportant and worthless. I also examined my motive in teaching and saw that it was not sincere desire to serve God but that I wanted an influential position and widespread recognition. I was in no doubt that I stood on an eroding sandbank, and was in imminent danger of hell-fire if I did not busy myself with mending my ways. . . .

[10] Gibb, *Mohammedanism*, p. 139.
[11] Quoted by W. Montgomery Watt, *Muslim Intellectual: a Study of al-Ghazali* (Edinburgh University Press, 1953), p. 135.

> I kept thinking about this for a time, as long as it remained a matter of choice. One day I would decide to leave Baghdad and escape from my involvements; the next day I would give up the decision. . . . Whenever morning found me with a genuine longing to seek the world to come, evening saw it reduced to nothing by the attack of a host of desires.[12]

After nearly six months of hesitation and vacillation, al-Ghazali tells us:

> The matter ceased to be one of choice and became one of necessity. God parched my tongue and I was prevented from teaching. I would make an effort to teach, . . . but my tongue would not utter a word. . . . My general health declined, and the physicians, realizing that the source of the trouble was in the heart, despaired of successful treatment, unless the anxiety of the heart could be relieved.
> Aware of my impotence and without the power of choice, I took refuge with God, driven to do so because I had no resource left.[13]

Resigning his posts in Baghdad and making provision for his family, al-Ghazali set forth as a solitary pilgrim on the Sufi path, first in Damascus, then on the hajj, and finally in his native Persia, where he settled down with a group of disciples.

Al-Ghazali now wrote his major work, *The Revival of the Religious Sciences.* Arguing from his own career, he warned that the concern of the ulema with the externals of the faith might lead to preoccupation with worldly matters at the expense of the spiritual. It was his conviction that both a scrupulous respect for the Sharia and the cultivation of the Sufi path were essential for salvation. Thus, as he himself had discovered, the two great aspects

[12] *Ibid.,* pp. 135–136.
[13] *Ibid.,* p. 137.

of religion—the theological and the mystical, or put another way, the institutional and the personal—not only could be reconciled but also were equally necessary and indispensable.

Al-Ghazali's place in the history of Islam may be compared with that of Augustine and Luther in Christianity, as Gibb has suggested. Al-Ghazali may be compared, too, with the medieval schoolmen, the Scholastic philosophers, who sought to extricate Christianity from the crisis precipitated by the study of Greek thought. Reason and faith were not antagonists but partners; reason, rightly understood, would buttress and not weaken faith.

PHILOSOPHY

The introduction to this book noted the existence in the West of two contrasting images of Islam, one deprecatory, the other often naively complimentary. Subsequent chapters have furnished instances where Western misunderstanding of Islamic achievements has made Muslims appear almost subhuman. In the present chapter and the next, discussing the Islamic reception of Greek ideas, we encounter the second image, with its exaggerated estimates of Islamic intellectual tolerance and originality that have made Muslims appear almost superhuman.

In the early twentieth century the respected Scottish scholar, Duncan B. Macdonald, claimed that under Hellenic influence a group of Muslim thinkers became

> daring and absolutely free-minded speculators. They were applying to the ideas of the Koran the keen solvent of Greek dialectic and the results which they obtained were of the most fantastically original character. Thrown into the wide sea and utter freedom of Greek thought, their ideas had expanded to the bursting point and, more than even a German metaphysician, they had lost touch of the ground of ordinary life, with its reasonable probabilities, and were swinging loose on a wild hunt after ultimate truth, wielding as their weapons definitions and syllogisms.[1]

More recent scholarship has dampened such extravagant claims. The high-flying intellectual speculators, von Grune-

---

[1] D. B. Macdonald, *Development of Muslim Theology, Jurisprudence and Constitutional Theory* (Premier Book House, 1960), pp. 139–140.

baum argues, may have borrowed from Greece and from other cultures; but "not a single borrowing proved effective, let alone lasting, unless Arabicized in terminology and cast into a familiar thought-pattern."[2] Although the caliph Mamun (A.D. 813–833), the son of the famous Harun ar-Rashid, subsidized a House of Wisdom to disseminate the "new learning," orthodox Islam soon silenced the most radical innovators.

The Greek Legacy

The new learning was founded on translations of Greek texts. Recent studies of Arabic manuscripts in European libraries as well as at Istanbul and Cairo indicate that during the Middle Ages more of the Greek legacy was accessible to the Islamic world than to Byzantium or Western Europe. Yet important gaps existed in Muslim knowledge of Greek works: the great dramas, for example, and most of the writings of the pre-Socratic philosophers were unavailable. Richard Walzer, a modern authority, concludes that the legacy of Greece to medieval Islam consisted essentially of what had been studied in the Greek schools that flourished in the days of the Roman Empire, several centuries after the golden age of Greece itself.

The Neoplatonists constituted the most influential school; as we have already seen, their mystical and gnostic teachings were readily assimilated into the larger syncretism of Shiism and Sufism. Also important were the Stoics, who preached cultivation of the virtues of self-discipline and endurance and who also believed in the force of natural law, a set of moral principles placed in the world of nature

[2] G. E. von Grunebaum, "Islam in a Humanistic Education," *Journal of Education*, vol. IV (1949), reprinted in J. Stewart-Robinson, ed., *The Traditional Near East* (Prentice-Hall, 1966), p. 51.

by its creator as a guide to men. Although Stoicism had originated in Greece during the fourth century B.C., its most famous spokesmen were distinguished Romans such as Cicero and Emperor Marcus Aurelius. A third school, the Epicurean, had also arisen in ancient Greece and received its most eloquent exposition from a Roman, the poet Lucretius. An agnostic, Lucretius denied the existence of an afterlife and argued therefore that men should spend their lives not in preparing for death but in cultivating the joys of the spirit and avoiding pain and despair.

The Hellenic content of the Greek legacy underwent significant dilution because most Muslims read Greek texts in a translation or, frequently, in a translation of a translation. By the fifth century A.D. many Greek works were being rendered in Syriac (a form of Aramaic), and it was often these Syriac versions that were later rendered into Arabic. In both cases the translators were almost invariably Christians, usually Monophysites or Nestorians rather than Orthodox. Their involvement in the heresies that convulsed the early Byzantine world colored their translations, much as nineteenth-century English translations of the Greek classics were to be colored by Victorian moral concerns. Richard Walzer puts the matter persuasively:

> Translators are not very conspicuous figures in the history of philosophy, but without their painstaking work the essential links in the continuity of Western thought would never have been forged, nor would Arabic philosophy in particular ever have come into existence. The function of these translators was not simply to transmit texts. Working partly under the influence of the Arabic theologians, but to a greater extent on their own initiative, they were instrumental in building up a complex and lucid Arabic philosophical terminology and laying the foundations for a philosophical Arabic style. This terminology reproduces the terminology of the late Greek commentators and of the Neoplatonic philosophers

which had gone far beyond Aristotle and Plato themselves.[3]

Determinism and Free Will

The ulema turned to Arabized Hellenic concepts in
dealing with the opposing arguments raised by the champions of determinism and the champions of free will. At
the head of the latter group were the Kharijites. These
ardent puritans, whom we have already met (pp. 71–72),
believed that the man who sinned did so out of his free
choice and should no longer be considered a Muslim at
all, and could therefore become the object of jihad. The
Kharijites judged men not only by the intensity of their
faith but by the quality of their works, their deeds. Regarding caliphs such as Ali and the early Umayyads as
unworthy, the Kharijites refused to acknowledge the legitimacy of the caliphate and regarded themselves as a
kind of community of saints.

Critics of the Kharijites went to the other extreme,
arguing that God predetermined men's deeds, that a man's
faith mattered more than his works, and that an established regime should be supported as part of God's handiwork. These critics were known as Murjiites ("postponers"),
because they believed that ultimate judgment on a man's
worthiness should be postponed to the Last Day. They
held out the hope that sinners might gain eventual ad-
mittance to paradise after expiating some of their sins by
a sojourn in hell.

The Mutazilites

Some ulema, although hostile to the Kharijites, also
had great misgivings about the diminution of man's re-

[3] Richard Walzer, *Greek into Arabic: Essays on Islamic Philosophy* (Harvard University Press, 1962), pp. 7–8.

sponsibility for his own behavior implicit in Murjiite teachings. Seeking a middle way between opposing extremes,
these ulema were styled Mutazilites, a name suggesting
those who were neutral or who abstained. It was the
Mutazilites whom Macdonald had in mind when he wrote
the exuberant passage on Muslim Hellenizers quoted earlier
in this chapter; he viewed their sponsorship by the caliph
Mamun as the prelude to a new era of liberalism and
tolerance, unhappily aborted by their subsequent fall from
grace under the caliphs of the later ninth century. Recent
studies have exploded the concept that the Mutazilites
were the freethinkers of Islam and have challenged their
reputation for liberalism. In the heyday of official favor
they were as arbitrary and intolerant as the reactionaries
whom they attacked; they were responsible for having
Ahmad ibn-Hanbal, founder of the fundamentalist Hanbali
interpretation of the Sharia, flogged and sent to prison because he attacked their Greek way of reasoning as un-
Muslim.

It is now generally agreed that the Mutazilites had
recourse to Greek philosophy not as an end in itself but as
a means of strengthening Islam. They feared erosion from
within by the spread of gnosticism and the Shia cult of
the godlike Ali and from such external threats to pure
monotheism as trinitarian Christianity. It was particularly
to counter gnostic stress on secrecy and magic that they
borrowed Aristotelian methods of argument, thereby opening themselves to the charge that they put too much stress
on reason as a way to truth and too little on revelation.

The Mutazilites especially deplored what they considered to be the anthropomorphic concepts of Allah that
had crept into the faith since the days of the Prophet. In
defending what they termed the *unity of God,* they argued
that the ninety-nine most beautiful names assigned far too
much importance to his human attributes. The Mutazilites
also questioned the literal interpretation of Koranic refer-

ences to the speech of God, to his face, and to his sitting on a throne and engaging in other seemingly human activities. Whereas the Mutazilites' concept of the unity of God transcended human limitations, their explanation of the justice of God seemed to place limits on his power. Borrowing from Stoic philosophy, they argued that the natural law of morality implanted in the universe by God obliged him to reward the virtuous and punish the wicked. This doctrine was sometimes called that of *promise and threat:* God had to make good his promise of heaven and threat of hell; he had to preserve men's free will, their capacity to choose between good and evil courses.

The majority of Muslims could not accept Mutazilite teachings. The doctrine of promise and threat made God subject to human standards, thereby denying his omnipotence; the doctrine of the unity of God contradicted the explicit statements of the Koran on God's attributes and therefore suggested that the Koran itself, the speech of Allah, was not eternal but something less authoritative and majestic. It seemed to most of the faithful that the Mutazilites were elevating reason above revelation and were denaturing God in their attempts to bridge the gulf between the human and the divine.

Rejection of Mutazilism occurred first on the political level, about the middle of the ninth century, when the successors of Mamun abandoned his unsuccessful efforts to impose the new teachings. On the intellectual and theological level the struggle continued into the next century, as the more moderate Mutazilite ulema gradually returned to traditional theology. Their return is symbolized by a famous story, illustrating the absurdity of attempts to explain the justice of God in human terms:

'Let us imagine a child and a grown-up in Heaven who both died in the True Faith, but the grown-up has a higher place than the child. And the child will ask God, "Why did you give that man a higher place?" And God will answer, "He has done many good works." Then the child will say, "Why did you let me die so soon so that I was prevented from doing good?" God will answer, "I knew that you would grow up a sinner, therefore, it was better that you should die a child." Then a cry goes up from the damned in the depths of Hell, "Why, O Lord, did you not let us die before we became sinners?" '4

The former Mutazilite ulema were called Asharites, after their leader, Abul-Hasan al-Ashari (A.D. 873–935), who refuted the stubborn Mutazilites on their own terms by arguing from reason. In answer to the Mutazilites' defense of the unity of God al-Ashari claimed that God did exercise functions attributed to him, such as seeing and speaking, but men could not hope to understand their nature. He further contended that there were no restrictions on the justice of God, who caused both good and evil to exist and endowed men with the power to choose between the two; thus, in effect, human free will existed within a larger framework of determinism. Although the Asharites overcame Mutazilite opposition with relative ease, they had more difficulty with conservatives like the Hanbali ulema, who deplored their appeals to rationalism. Official recognition came only during the era of Seljuk dominance in the later eleventh century; thereafter Asharism was to remain the orthodox theology of Sunni Islam for the rest of the Middle Ages.

The Philosophers: Ar-Razi

An important champion of the Asharites in their successful struggle with the Hanbali ulema was the great intellectual and mystic al-Ghazali. Yet, as we have already seen (pp. 108–111), al-Ghazali ultimately denounced the incoherence of philosophy and turned from rationalism to

4 Quoted in S. van den Bergh, trans., *Averroes' Tahafut al-Tahafut*, I (Luzac, 1954), p. x. Permission by Gibb Memorial Trust.

the Sufi way. Other examples of the unsettling effects produced by the new learning on Muslim intellectuals will now be encountered as we survey some representative medieval Islamic philosophers. They reached no consensus on the great issues of faith and reason comparable to that of the Asharites in theology; their conclusions were as diverse as their geographical backgrounds, which stretched from Spain and North Africa to Iraq, Persia, and Central Asia. One of them, at least, was better qualified than the Mutazilites to be called a freethinker of Islam: ar-Razi (c.a.d. 865–c.923), the man from Rayy, an ancient Persian town near modern Tehran.

Famous as a physician and teacher, ar-Razi studied Platonic, Stoic, and Epicurean philosophy and took as his hero Socrates, the great questioner of established ideas and values. Ar-Razi's questioning led him to doubt the validity of religious teachings and caused orthodox Muslims to destroy his philosophical writings. When cataracts eventually made him blind, it was widely assumed that they were Allah's judgment upon him for impiety. His rationalist and skeptical temper of mind may be glimpsed in his delightful essay, "The Spiritual Physick," composed as a companion piece to a compendium of medical lore. He sings the praises of reason, which, he wrote,

> is God's greatest blessing to us. . . . Reason is the thing without which our state would be the state of wild beasts, of children and lunatics. . . . Since this is its worth and place, . . . it behooves us not to bring it down from its high rank or in any way to degrade it. . . . We must not give Passion the mastery over it, for Passion is the blemish of Reason . . . preventing the reasonable man from finding the true guidance and the ultimate salvation of all his affairs. . . . We must discipline and subject our Passion, driving and compelling it to obey the every dictate of Reason.[5]

[5] A. J. Arberry, trans., *The Spiritual Physick of Rhazes* (John Murray, 1950), pp. 20–21.

What leads men to give passion the upper hand is their fear of death, a subject on which ar-Razi's views reflect the agnosticism of Lucretius. If you believe that both body and soul perish when you die, he argues, then you should welcome death as a final release from the pains and frustrations of life. If you believe that the soul survives in an afterlife, then God will reward those who have observed religious law and be charitable to those who have not. In either case, there will be no terrible Day of Judgment such as that forecast in the Koran. "It is superfluous to grieve over what must inevitably come to pass," ar-Razi wrote. "For speculation on death brings upon us many times greater pain" than that to be anticipated at death, so that he "who imagines death, and is afraid of it, dies a separate death at every image he calls up."[6]

Al-Farabi

Ar-Razi's contemporary, al-Farabi (c. a.d. 870–950), a Turk from central Asia, came to be called *the second master* because he seemed a worthy successor of Aristotle. Nestorian Christian scholars and translators in Baghdad introduced him to the works of Aristotle, on which he wrote extensive commentaries. Al-Farabi was the first Islamic philosopher to put much stress on politics and, following Greek precedents, classified political entities by size—the *medina*, equivalent to the Greek city-state; the *umma*, or nation; and a universal state, a kind of enlarged caliphate. Each had a characteristic good form and bad form of government, on the pattern of the celebrated classification in Aristotle's *Politics*. Yet al-Farabi's interest in politics seems to have involved less of an Aristotelian analysis of things-as-they-are and more of a Platonic concern for things-as-they-ought-to-be. The ideal state sketched

[6] Arberry, *The Spiritual Physick of Rhazes*, pp. 105–106.

in al-Farabi's *Virtuous City* was to be the instrument for
attaining the good life; and its head was to be a moral
superman, combining the qualities of the Sunni caliph, the
Shiite imam, and the philosopher-king of Plato's *Republic*.

Although al-Farabi was a highly influential teacher,
his position in Islamic intellectual history remains a matter
of controversy because few of his writings are available in
scholarly editions and information about his career is frag-
mentary. For example, it is known that he worked with
Nestorians in Baghdad and later lived for a time at the
court of Shiite princes in Aleppo, in northern Syria; but we
do not know the extent to which he absorbed Christian
or Shiite doctrines. His own terminology is abstract (he
called the leader of his ideal state simply *the head*), and
writings from earlier and from later periods of his life express apparently contradictory views on Aristotelianism and
Platonism.

In consequence, we are left with a series of questions. Was al-Farabi's Platonism closer to The Republic
itself or to the gnosticism of the Neoplatonists? Did he have
the skepticism that led ar-Razi to rank reason above religion, or was his first allegiance to Islam? Did he Hellenize
and Christianize Islam, or did he, rather, make the Greek
and Christian legacies more Muslim? Was his ideal political
"head" more a philosopher-king or more a prophet? To
each of these questions one reputable scholar may be found
answering "yes," and another, equally reputable, replying
"no." The sharply differing assessments of al-Farabi are a
warning of the difficulties in bringing the image of the
Muslim intellectual into focus.[7]

---

[7] A cross-section of judgments on al-Farabi may be found in
Richard Walzer's article on him in *The Encyclopaedia of Islam*, new
ed. s.v. al-Farabi, in the introduction to Muhsin Mahdi's translation
of *Al-Farabi's Philosophy of Plato and Aristotle* (Free Press, 1962),
and in E. I. J. Rosenthal, *Political Thought in Medieval Islam*
(Cambridge University Press, 1958), chap. VI.

Avicenna

Luckily, the greatest of Muslim philosophers, Avicenna (ibn-Sina in Arabic, A.D. 980–1037), left an autobiography that conveys a sharply etched image of a remarkable personality. Born near Bukhara in Central Asia, probably of Persian descent, Avicenna described some of the highlights of his education:

> By the time I was ten I had mastered the Koran and a great deal of literature, so that I was marvelled at for my aptitude. . . . Now my father was one of those who had responded to the Egyptian propagandist (who was an Ismaili); he, and my brother too, had listened to what they say about the Spirit and the Intellect. . . . They would therefore discuss these things together, whilst I listened and comprehended all that they said; but my spirit would not assent to their argument. . . . Then there came to Bukhara a man . . . who claimed to be a philosopher; my father invited him to stay in our house, hoping that I would learn from him also. . . . He marvelled at me exceedingly, and warned my father that I should not engage in any other occupation but learning. Whatever problem he stated to me, I showed a better mental conception of it than he.
>
> I now occupied myself with mastering the various texts and commentaries on natural science and metaphysics. . . . Next I desired to study medicine, and proceeded to read all the books that have been written on this subject. Medicine is not a difficult science, and naturally I excelled in it in a very short time. . . . At the same time I continued between whiles to study and dispute on law, being now sixteen years of age.[8]

The child prodigy grew into a still more prodigious adult, a kind of Muslim anticipation of the universal man of the Renaissance so admired in the West a few centuries

8 A. J. Arberry, ed., *Aspects of Islamic Civilization* (Allen & Unwin, 1964), pp. 136–137. Permission by A. S. Barnes & Co.

later. Throwing himself into the rough and tumble of life, he served as both physician and prime minister to various princely rulers in Persia. Reportedly dictating on horseback in the course of official journeys, he produced an impressive list of writings, including a general encyclopedia of knowledge reputed to be the longest work of its kind by a single author.

Yet even an intellectual genius had his limitations. Avicenna relates that during his studies of logic, "Whenever I found myself perplexed by a problem, . . . I would repair to the mosque and pray, adoring the All-Creator, until my puzzle was resolved and my difficulty made easy."[9] The student's recourse to prayer forecasts the adult philosopher's endeavors to show that the truths arrived at by reason were compatible with those coming from revelation. Two characteristic arguments of Avicenna hinged on the *necessary being* and the *suspended man*.

The *necessary being* he defines as that "which when supposed to be not existing, an impossibility occurs from it,"[10] whereas no such impossibility occurs from the existence or nonexistence of a possible being. God, he concludes, is the necessary being, the creator of the process that enables possible beings to exist. The *suspended man* Avicenna imagines to be

a man created . . . in perfect bodily condition, but whose eyes are screened so as to prevent him from perceiving external things. Imagine further that this man floats in the empty air in such a manner that he has no sensation, not even such as may be caused by the touch and friction of the air.[11]

[9] Arberry, *Aspects of Islamic Civilization,* p. 138.
[10] Soheil M. Afnan, *Avicenna* (Allen & Unwin, 1958), pp. 123–124.
[11] Quoted by J. L. Teicher, "Avicenna's Place in Arabic Philosophy," in G. Wickens, ed., *Avicenna: Scientist and Philosopher* (Luzac, 1952), p. 39.

Although such a man can see and feel nothing external, he is nevertheless aware of his own mind and soul. The argument is very like that advanced six centuries later by Descartes—"I think, therefore I am"; a man can doubt everything except the fact that in performing the act of doubting he exists. In a famous poem Avicenna puts the case more in the manner of the Sufis, comparing the soul to a dove sent by God to live in a mean earthly body and grieve over her exile until at last freed to return home:

> Why then was she cast down from her high peak
> To this degrading depth? God brought her low,
> But for a purpose wise, that is concealed
> E'en from the keenest mind and liveliest wit.
> And if the tangled mesh impeded her,
> The narrow cage denied her wings to soar
> Freely in heaven's high ranges, after all
> She was a lightning flash that brightly glowed
> Momently o'er the tents, and then was hid
> As though its gleam was never glimpsed below.[12]

Avicenna's rationalism and mysticism alike have drawn both praise and criticism. Al-Ghazali, for example, attacks him in *The Incoherence of Philosophy* for failing to sense that the man who reasoned could never hope to find the Sufi path to God, whereas Averroes, a Spanish Muslim philosopher, denounced al-Ghazali's attack and deplored Avicenna's lapses into mysticism. From Spain the influence of Avicenna's writings in Latin translation extended to Catholic Europe. There Saint Thomas Aquinas, greatest of the Scholastic philosophers, turned to Avicenna's necessary being for a rational proof of God's existence and also for help in resolving the disputes that raged in the West over the nature of universals. A universal was the *idea* of something in general, a chair or table, rather than

---

[12] A. J. Arberry, "Avicenna: His Life and Times," in Wickens, *Avicenna: Scientist and Philosopher* p. 28.

a three-dimensional article, or, for another example, the genus horse, rather than a flesh-and-blood horse of a particular breed. The nominalists, who argued that such universals were merely convenient names, seemed guilty of materialism; the realists, who contended that the universal or genus had a higher reality, seemed to belittle the importance of individual specimens or objects in the material world. By the kind of reasoning that the French call *avicennisant* ("Avicennizing"), the Scholastics were able to argue that the universal was a concept, more than a name yet without an existence of its own apart from specific instances.

Averroes

Averroes (in Arabic, ibn-Rushd, 1126–1198) made the last great medieval effort to reconcile reason with Islam. A respected member of the ulema and a Malikite judge at Cordova, Averroes was also a devotee of the new learning and a profound Aristotelian scholar, who pruned away some of the Neoplatonic teachings that had been wrongly attributed to Aristotle by earlier Islamic scholars. His conviction of the fundamental harmony of philosophy and religion impelled him to write a treatise with that title. And to rebut the anti-rationalist strictures of al-Ghazali's *Incoherence of Philosophy*, he wrote *The Incoherence of the Incoherence*, demonstrating that reason, too, could lead to the truths supposedly reserved for the Sufi.

Yet the achievement of Averroes, impressive though it was, marked an end rather than a beginning. Distracted by the Christian reconquest of the peninsula and by the disintegration of Muslim political power, the world of Spanish Islam was becoming increasingly inhospitable to intellectual activity. In the Muslim east, the prevalence of Asharite theology in the official world and of Sufism in that of popular religion also created a climate hostile to intellectual innovation. Averroes did, however, play a major role in the history of Western philosophy, in part through his clarification of Aristotle's thought and in part because many Catholics misunderstood his doctrine of harmony and supposed that he preached the ascendancy of philosophy over religion. *Averroism* became a synonym for heresy. There is irony as well as truth in the claim that Averroes "can, in a sense, be regarded as belonging even more to the philosophical tradition of the West, than to the mainstream of the intellectual life of Islam."[13]

Ibn-Khaldun

The twilight centuries of medieval Islamic civilization produced one other great intellectual figure, the historian and philosopher, ibn-Khaldun (1332–1406). Born in Tunisia of a refugee Arab family from Spain, he received a thorough grounding in law and theology and acquired a valuable practical apprenticeship as tutor or minister to various princes in North Africa and Granada. As middle age approached, he withdrew from the chaos and uncertainties of politics and, after a long period of writing in seclusion, moved to Egypt. In Mameluk Cairo he was a teacher at al-Azhar and a judge in the courts of Maliki law, where he won a reputation for exceptional severity. A few years before his death he spent an interval in Damascus at the court of the meteoric Tatar conqueror, Tamerlane.

The flux and decay that ibn-Khaldun witnessed in his youth prompted him to examine in detail the nature and causes of these phenomena. He pursued the project for many years; and as a prelude to a multivolumed universal

[13] Seyyed Hossein Nasr, *Science and Civilization in Islam* (Harvard University Press, 1968), p. 317.

history he composed the three volumes of the *Muqaddimah*, or introduction, on which his fame chiefly rests. In it he expounds what he terms a *new science* and what his modern admirers proclaim to be a pioneering philosophy of history. Here are some of its essential qualities:

> We say that man is distinguished from other living beings by certain qualities peculiar to him, namely: (1) The sciences and crafts which result from that ability to think which distinguishes him from the other animals and exalts him as a thinking being over all creatures. (2) The need for restraining influence and strong authority, since man, alone of all the animals, cannot exist without them. . . . (3) Man's efforts to make a living and his concern with the various ways of obtaining and acquiring the means of life. . . . (4) Civilization. This means that human beings have to dwell in common and settle together in cities and hamlets for the comforts of companionship and for the satisfaction of human needs, as the result of the natural disposition of human beings toward co-operation in order to be able to make a living.[14]

When ibn-Khaldun amplifies these four qualities, his new science often incorporates older wisdom from the Koran and the Sharia. But he also shows fresh insights, particularly when he examines a subject on which he had much first-hand information and sums up the reasons why the life span of a political dynasty is only three generations:

> The first generation retains the desert qualities, desert toughness, and desert savagery. Its members are used to privation and to sharing their glory with each other; they are brave and rapacious. Therefore, the strength of group feeling continues to be preserved among them. . . .
> Under the influence of royal authority and a life of ease, the second generation changes from the desert

14 Ibn-Khaldun, *The Muqaddimah*, abridged, trans. F. Rosenthal, (Princeton University Press, 1969), pp. 42–43.

attitude to sedentary culture, from privation to luxury
and plenty, from a state in which everybody shared in
the glory to one in which one man claims all the glory
for himself. . . . Thus the vigour of group feeling is
broken to some extent. People become used to lowliness
and obedience. But many of the old virtues remain in
them. . . .

The third generation, then, has completely for-
gotten the period of desert life and toughness, as if it
had never existed. They have lost the taste for the
sweetness of fame and for group feeling, because they
are dominated by force. Luxury reaches its peak among
them, because they are so much given to a life of prosperity and ease. They became dependent on the dynasty
and are like women and children who need to be defended. Group feeling disappears completely.[15]

The prominence that ibn-Khaldun gives to group feeling or
solidarity has done much to earn him the reputation as
the first social psychologist or sociologist. The *Muqaddimah*
has been called "one of the solemn moments of human
thought" and its author a "solitary genius" who "had no
forerunners among Arabic writers," and "no successors or
emulators in this idiom until the contemporary period."[16]

[15] *Ibid.*, p. 137.
[16] *The Encyclopaedia of Islam*, new ed., s.v. ibn-Khaldun.

SCIENCE

Several of the great names in Islamic philosophy—ar-Razi, al-Farabi, Avicenna—also figure prominently in the history of Islamic science. Scientists, too, built on the work of older civilizations, Greek, Persian, Hindu, and even Chinese (it is possible that the Arabic word *alchemy* is derived from the Chinese for *gold-extracting juice*). In science as in philosophy, many of the men responsible for transmitting older traditions were non-Muslims; Christians translated Greek works, and in Baghdad certain Christian and Jewish families, generation after generation, supplied the physicians and pharmacists who served the upper classes.

The extremely important contributions made by non-Muslims to Islamic culture suggest that in this context the term *Islamic* has such broad and syncretistic implications that, unlike *Muslim,* it does not necessarily refer to participation in a particular religious faith. Some historians refer to the Abbasid caliphate as the *Islamic empire* to point up the contrast between its cosmopolitanism and the more primitive, more soldierly, and predominantly Muslim qualities of the Umayyads' *Arab kingdom.* Medieval Spain furnished striking examples of a kind of cultural free trade between Muslims and non-Muslims. The Jew Maimonides (1134–1204) is a significant personage in the Islamic tradition because he was physician to Saladin, wrote in Arabic not Hebrew, and carried forward the philosophical inquiries of his master, Averroes. Jews and Christians participated significantly in the intellectual and scientific life of Toledo, which continued almost without interruption after the city passed permanently from Muslim to Christian control in 1085. In the twelfth and thirteenth centuries the archbishops of Toledo, the ranking prelates of Spain, made the city far and away the most important center for translating works by Muslim intellectuals into Latin.

The linguistic preeminence of Arabic and the relative ease of travel across the length and breadth of the medieval Islamic world permitted the development of important scientific centers all the way from Spain and Morocco to Samarkand in Central Asia, capital of the conqueror Tamerlane, who established a great school there at the close of the Middle Ages. In the first two Muslim centuries the major scientific center was the city of Jundishapur in southwestern Persia, founded by the Sasanid emperor Shapur, who defeated the legions of Rome in the third century A.D. Renowned for its hospital and its medical and scientific academies, Jundishapur attracted many Nestorian refugees from Byzantine persecution. Under the early Abbasid caliphs leadership passed to Baghdad, where the caliphs' House of Wisdom established a vigorous intellectual tradition continued by the city's schools and hospitals. In the tenth and eleventh centuries the energy of the Ismaili movement and the patronage of the Fatimid caliphs, particularly in establishing a great library, brought Cairo to the first rank. It remained there during many later political vicissitudes thanks to the continuity provided by institutions such as its famous hospitals and the university of al-Azhar.

Medicine

In the medieval Islamic world the medical profession was established and recognized to a degree unknown in Catholic Europe. Reputable physicians were on the whole highly esteemed and well paid; an outstanding doctor such as Avicenna served Persian princes not only as a physician but also as a political counsellor. The starting point of Islamic medicine was the legacy of Hindu and Persian medical lore preserved at Jundishapur, supplemented by the Arabic translation of the Greek physician Galen, who had summarized the medical legacy of the ancient Mediterranean world in the second century A.D.

Past authorities did not necessarily command uncritical deference from Muslim physicians. For example, ar-Razi, who flourished about A.D. 900, cited Greek, Syriac, Persian, and Hindu opinions on a given question and then presented his own views. This independent attitude enabled ar-Razi to make some important discoveries, above all to distinguish for the first time the differences between smallpox and measles. Here is an excerpt from his monograph on these two diseases:

> The outbreak of small-pox is preceded by continuous fever, aching in the back, itching in the nose and shivering during sleep. The main symptoms of its presence are: back-ache with fever, stinging pain in the whole body, congestion of the face, sometimes shrinkage, violent redness of the cheeks and eyes, a sense of pressure in the body, creeping of the flesh, pain in the throat and breast accompanied by difficulty of respiration and coughing, dryness of the mouth, thick salivation, hoarseness of the voice, headache and pressure in the head, excitement, anxiety, nausea and unrest. Excitement, nausea and unrest are more pronounced in measles than in small-pox, whilst the aching in the back is more severe in small-pox than in measles.[1]

Through careful detailed observation, ar-Razi added much to the store of clinical data about infectious diseases that had been accumulating since the pioneering work of Hippocrates 1300 years earlier.

[1] Quoted by Max Meyerhof, "Science and Medicine," in T. Arnold and A. Guillaume, eds., *The Legacy of Islam* (London: Oxford University Press, 1931), pp. 323–324.

Ar-Razi's contribution to Islamic medicine was the more remarkable because he only began his studies in middle age, when he already had many other intellectual irons in the fire. He directed a hospital in his native Rayy, then another at Baghdad, and wrote more than fifty clinical studies in addition to more ambitious general works. The latter included the *Comprehensive Book*, the longest medical work in the Arabic language (over eighteen volumes in an incomplete modern edition), which Renaissance Europeans much respected in its Latin translation. In the present century ar-Razi has attracted attention because of his *Spiritual Physick* (see pp. 109–110) and other original works on the psychological and sociological aspects of medicine. A few pertinent titles are: *On the Fact That Even Skillful Physicians Cannot Heal All Diseases; Why Frightened Patients Easily Forsake Even the Skilled Physician; Why People Prefer Quacks and Charlatans.*

A hundred years later, Avicenna also placed considerable stress on psychosomatic medicine and reportedly was able to cure a prince suffering from a severe depression. The patient imagined himself to be a cow, made lowing noises, and demanded to be butchered and converted into stew beef; Avicenna, posing as a cheerful butcher, refused to oblige, claiming that the intended victim was too scrawny and needed to be fattened up; whereupon the patient began eating heartily and eventually recovered his health. Avicenna compiled an encyclopedia, *The Canon of Medicine*, which was more systematic than Razi's *Comprehensive Book* and was widely consulted in the Arab world down to the last century and in Western Europe until the 1600s. Avicenna appears to have been the first doctor to describe and identify meningitis and the first to recommend alcohol as a disinfectant.

The more scholars examine the sources, the more "firsts" can be claimed for Islamic medicine. The work of Avicenna and others on eye diseases, very prevalent in the

Middle East, and on the nature of vision helped to found the study of optics. These studies also made possible rather complicated operations on the eye. Muslim surgeons used opium for anesthesia and attempted experimental operations, including the extraction of teeth and their replacement by ones made from animal bones, the removal of kidney stones lodged in the bladder, and possibly even colostomy (opening of an artificial anus after removal of cancerous tissue).

However, it is important to keep a proper perspective on Islamic medical achievements and not to magnify them unduly. Mortality among surgical patients appears to have been very high, because doctors knew little about either antiseptic measures or the details of anatomy. Muslim tradition forbade dissecting corpses, though a little clandestine dissection may have occurred, mainly in Spain. Some scholars, therefore, discount reports that a thirteenth-century Egyptian physician discovered the existence of the pulmonary circulation, which accounts for the passage of the blood from one chamber of the heart to another via the lungs. He may have advanced this theory three centuries before it was confirmed by European scientists; but it was a purely speculative hypothesis, untested clinically or experimentally.

Mathematics and the Physical Sciences

To describe certain procedures mathematicians borrowed from the vocabulary of surgery the term *al-jabr*, meaning restoration or reestablishment of something broken (Spaniards still call a bone-setter an *algebrista*). Islamic algebra was built on Greek and Hindu foundations and closely linked to geometry; its principal architects were the ninth-century Zoroastrian, al-Khuwarizmi, and the twelfth-century Persian, Omar Khayyam. Al-Khuwarizmi, who worked at the House of Wisdom in Baghdad, wrote a very influential book on algebra and also contributed to the development of trigonometry. He described an angle by an Arabic word meaning *pocket* or *pouch,* which was translated into the Latin *sinus*—whence our *sine.* Omar Khayyam, who was also a poet and a Sufi as well as an astronomer, is an excellent instance of the Muslim who sought both the rationalist and the gnostic paths to truth. Indeed, many Islamic mathematicians, like the Pythagoreans of ancient Greece, believed that through numbers men could ascend beyond the world of bewildering phenomena into a higher realm of abstractions and eternal verities. Because the science of numbers was regarded as "the tongue which speaks of unity and transcendence," it was appropriate to use as charms magic squares based on the numerical value of some of the ninety-nine names of God.

To the average Westerner, Arabic numbers have the merit of great simplicity, in contrast to the cumbersome Roman system based on letters. The simplicity of the Arabic system, however, is somewhat deceptive. The numerals used in the West, except for 1 and 9, do not look much like those used today by Arabs and Persians: their numerals are derived from those used in medieval Iraq, whereas ours come through medieval Spain. All of them, except for zero, almost certainly go back ultimately to the Hindus. The most revolutionary innovation of Arabic numbers was not their greater convenience, valuable and time-saving though this was; it lay in the Arabs' use of a dot to indicate an empty column, ten, for example, being 1·, one hundred one 1·1, and one million and one 1·····1. The dot was called *sifr* ("empty"), whence our *cipher* and, through an Italian translation, our *zero.* This system made possible a whole new world of arithmetical operations.

Islamic mathematicians opened new worlds to science, or at least freshened understanding of older worlds.

Increased knowledge of geometry and algebra aided the development of optics. The tables compiled by observers systematically recording their findings were utilized by later astronomers both in the Islamic world and in Europe. Islamic advances in trigonometry allowed computations that refined the picture of the earth-centered universe drawn by Ptolemy, the Greco-Egyptian astronomer of the second century A.D. One such refinement disclosed the eccentric behavior of Venus, which would have been easier to explain if the planet had been viewed as orbiting around the sun rather than around the earth. But, as in the medieval West, acceptance of the Ptolemaic system was too ingrained to countenance such a radical innovation as the heliocentric universe.

In certain instances theoretical science was turned to practical account. Astronomical tables enabled the faithful to determine the direction of Mecca and to schedule the five daily prayers and fix the annual festivals and holy days of the lunar calendar. Astronomy and geography facilitated navigation of the monsoon-swept Indian ocean, and mathematics and physics encouraged improvement of water clocks and of water wheels and other irrigation apparatus. Mechanical devices were sometimes remarkably ingenious, as in this thirteenth-century clock consisting of an elephant and a fantastic contrivance mounted on its back:

> Every half-hour the bird on top of the cupola whistles and turns while the mahout hits the elephant with his pick-axe and sounds a tattoo with his drumstick. In addition, the little man who seems to be looking out of a window . . . moves his arms and legs to induce the falcon below to release a pellet. This moving downward, makes the dragon turn until it is finally ejected into the little vase on the elephant's back. From there it drops into the animal, hits a gong, and finally comes to rest in a little bowl where the observer can establish the

half-hours passed by counting the number of little balls collected there.[2]

Astrology and Alchemy

Modern Westerners, who are amused by the talent expended on such fanciful gadgets, are uneasy when they learn that many Islamic astronomers were also astrologers and that a pioneer psychologist and physician such as ar-Razi could also be an alchemist. Astrology is based on the belief that the universe is, as the name suggests, a totality in which the stars do determine and indeed predestine activities on earth. Alchemy is based on the theory that there is a hierarchy of metals, from the base to the pure; if man can find the magical philosopher's stone or elixir, he will be able to change one to the other, iron to gold, or lead to silver, and perhaps also to make glass or quartz into emeralds or some other precious stone.

To us today all this seems an unfortunate confusion between true science and occult or pseudo science; our medieval forebears accepted the occult as a matter of course. Ancient traditions, together with the gnostic elements present in both Christianity and Islam, nourished the widely held conviction that there were other pathways to truth beside the one that we call rationalist or scientific. The more radical Shiites, especially the Ismailis with their concern for discovering the hidden message of the Koran, endeavored to unlock the secrets of nature by esoteric means as well as by scientific ones. The Sufis strove to release themselves from the physical restraints of body and mind to enable the soul to penetrate the veils concealing God.

A modern Persian scholar, familiar both with the history of science and with the Shii and Sufi traditions, advances this explanation for the popularity of alchemy:

[2] Richard Ettinghausen, *Arab Painting* (World, 1962), p. 95.

We must remember that ancient and medieval man did
not separate the material order from the psychological and
spiritual in the categorical manner that has become
customary today. There was a "naiveness" in the mental-
ity of premodern man which made it possible for him
. . . to see a deeper significance in physical phenomena
than just plain facts. . . . The basic symbols and principles of alchemy stem from the earliest periods of history
and convey through their very concreteness the primor-
dial character of this point of view. Ancient man, during
the millennia before recorded history, considered metals
to be a special class of beings, which did not belong to
the natural environment of the "Adamic race." The
earliest iron probably came from meteorites which, in
falling from the heavens, gave that metal special virtues
and powers.[3]

Although this hypothesis is controversial, there seems little
doubt that alchemy was regarded as a quasi-religious pur-
suit. It has been argued that, just as the alchemist sought
to transmute baser metals into gold, so he also sought a
kind of transmutation of the soul, which would release it
from the sin imposed by the fall of Adam from Eden and
allow it to reach a nobler state. The alchemist has likewise
been compared to a Sufi sheik, guiding his disciples on
their way to God, and to the Christian priest, celebrating
the miracle of the mass, which transforms the bread and
wine into the body and blood of Christ.

Astrology and alchemy were, in effect, the face and
obverse of the same coin, the one turned toward the
heavens and the other toward the earth. The seven metals
of the alchemist were the earthly symbols of the astrologer's
seven planets—gold symbolized the sun, silver the moon,
quicksilver Mercury, copper Venus, iron Mars, tin Jupiter,
and lead Saturn. From the ancient Greeks Islamic alchemists borrowed the concept of four fundamental ele-

[3] Seyyed Hossein Nasr, *Science and Civilization in Islam*
(Harvard University Press, 1968), p. 243.

ments—fire, air, earth, and water. Each of these, they argued, combined two of the four fundamental character- istics or qualities of nature, heat, cold, dryness, and wet- ness: fire was hot and dry, air hot and wet, earth cold and dry, and water cold and wet.

Islamic physicians, also borrowing from the Greeks, put the four humors of the human body into this pattern, noting that each produced a characteristic temperament. Yellow bile, which was hot and dry, made a man fiery or choleric; blood, which was hot and wet, made him sanguine or cheerful; black bile, which was cold and dry, made him melancholy; and phlegm, cold and wet, made him phleg- matic. When the humors were reasonably balanced, the in- dividual was in good health. In illness, the balance was destroyed; and treatment consisted in prescribing for the patient drugs and a diet that would supply the humors in which he was deficient until his normal balance was re- stored.

The doctrines of astrology and alchemy did not win universal approval in the medieval Islamic world. The ulema proclaimed them contrary to the faith, and several distinguished philosophers rejected them as contrary to reason. Ibn-Khaldun concluded:

> The worthlessness of astrology from the point of view of the religious law, as well as the weakness of its achievements from the rational point of view, are evident. In addition, astrology does harm to human civilization. It hurts the faith of the common people when an astro- logical judgment occasionally happens to come true. . . . Ignorant people are taken in by that and suppose that all the other astrological judgments must be true.[4]

And Avicenna flatly denied the possibility of physical transmutation:

[4] Ibn-Khaldun, *The Muqaddimah,* abridged (Princeton Uni- versity Press, 1969), p. 408.

As to the claims of the alchemists, it must be clearly understood that it is not in their power to bring about any true change of species. They can, however, produce excellent imitations, dyeing the red metal white so that it resembles silver, or dyeing it yellow so that it closely resembles gold. They can, too, dye the white metal with any colour they desire, until it bears a close resemblance to gold or copper; and they can free the leads from most of their defects and impurities. Yet in these dyed metals the essential nature remains unchanged.[5]

This last passage nevertheless suggests how the Arabic *al-kimiya* was to furnish modern chemistry both with its name and with some of its techniques and apparatus. In addition to being expert dyers, the alchemists developed methods of refining metals and of applying varnish to protect iron or waterproof cloth. They employed such chemical processes as distillation, evaporation, sublimation, crystallization, and filtration. Ar-Razi, in his writings on alchemy, describes vials, beakers, mortars and pestles, flasks, smelters, and other items of equipment. A modern scholar has compared the power attributed to the elusive philosopher's stone with that actually present in a chemical catalyst.[6]

Music

At first glance it seems strange that the quantitative sciences of the medieval Islamic curriculum should have included arithmetic, geometry, astronomy, optics—and music, a discipline that we tend to bracket with the arts and humanities. Yet the same list of subjects, except for

[5] Quoted in A. C. Crombie, "Avicenna's Influence on the Medieval Scientific Tradition," in G. M. Wickens, ed., *Avicenna: Scientist and Philosopher* (Luzac, 1952), p. 96.
[6] A. Mieli, *La Science Arabe et Son Rôle dans l'Evolution Scientifique Mondiale* (Brill, 1938), pp. 131–132.

optics, formed the quadrivium (fourfold way to knowledge) in the schools of the medieval West. Many of the leading Islamic scientists wrote on music—ar-Razi, who was a talented lute-player; Avicenna, who was an expert in rhythm; and, above all, al-Farabi, who compiled the *Grand Book of Music,* considered the most important work on musical theory written in the Middle Ages.

In theory Islamic musicians relied heavily on Pythagoras and other ancient Greeks and also on Byzantine and Persian precedents and on rhythmical early Arab poetry. Their greatest innovation was technical, indeed quantitative: it was a system of measures that assigned each sound a time value, in contrast to the unmeasured plain song of the early medieval West. Measures endowed music with greater structure, encouraged new concepts of rhythm, and ultimately led to the full, half, quarter, and other notes we use today. Islamic musicians applied mathematics to stringed instruments by the device of frets, which allowed the player to tune a string to a desired note. These musicians provided the West with the lute (in Arabic, *al-oud*), with the rebec, a pioneering two-stringed instrument played with a bow rather than plucked, and possibly with the guitar (*qitara* in Arabic), though the instrument, like its name, *kithara,* may have been of Greek origin. The tambourine ("little drum") is of Islamic origin, as is *fanfare,* a word derived from the Arabic for *trumpets* and reflecting Muslim enthusiasm for martial music.

Music had no recognized formal role in Islamic life. The chanting of Koranic passages and the intonation of prayers were not regarded as musical activities, and fundamentalists opposed free indulgence in music as conducive to debauchery and paganism. Al-Ghazali once recommended that the best way to disarm the temptations of secular music was to break the instruments used and rout the singers. Yet the same al-Ghazali wrote *Music and Ecstasy,* praising the contribution of music to the Sufi dhikr; and visitors to Konya may still hear the strains of flute, rebec, and drum to which the Mevlevi dervishes danced their way to a mystical trance.

In practice, then, music played an important informal role in Islamic life. It accompanied the recital of poetry, and it was recommended to relieve the distress of the ill or the depressed (musical therapy is not a twentieth-century invention). Music was a central ingredient in military and palace ceremonies; and it underscored the capers of jesters, which inspired those morris dances that sound so very English but were actually Moorish and performed by dancers with faces blackened to resemble Moors. Music illustrates once again the complexity of the Islamic tradition, the coexistence of the sacred and the profane, the gnostic and the scientific.

THE ARTS
AND LITERATURE

The medieval Christian West owed a debt to the art and literature of the Islamic world as well as to its thought and science. The pointed arch and arabesque tracery so prevalent in the Gothic architecture of the thirteenth and fourteenth centuries had been employed in mosques and Muslim palaces several hundred years before. The chivalric love poems sung by the troubadours at the court of Eleanor of Aquitaine in the twelfth century echoed Arabic lyrics from Spain, although just how faithful that echo was is still a matter of controversy among scholars. Islamic craftsmen and writers in their turn were indebted to the Copts of pre-Muslim Egypt, to the Romans and Byzantines, the Persians and Hindus. Islamic culture —"culture" in the layman's sense of something apart from the grubby workaday world rather than in the more comprehensive and materialistic usage of the anthropologist and the sociologist—forms part of a great continuum extending from remote antiquity to the present day.

Islamic culture displayed a distinctive style and personality of its own along with its cosmopolitan and timeless qualities. Early Islamic builders, while borrowing freely from older cultures to supplement primitive Arab architectural models, usually produced a structure that made a truly Islamic statement. For examples we may turn to the three earliest major Muslim monuments—the Dome of the Rock in Jerusalem (completed in A.D. 691), the al-Aqsa Mosque, also in Jerusalem, and the Great Mosque of Damascus (both dating from the early eighth century).

Three Early Monuments

Though often called the Mosque of Umar, after the caliph who conquered Jerusalem in the 630s, the Dome of the Rock was the work of the Umayyad Caliph Abd al-Malik, half a century later. More than a mosque, it is a unique political and religious monument, standing on the rocky summit of a small hill known as Mount Moriah, which marks the site of Solomon's Temple and, according to a Muslim legend, may also mark the place from which Muhammad mounted a ladder to visit heaven during a visionary night journey. In the hope that the Dome of the Rock would supplant the Meccan Kaaba as the central focus of Muslim veneration, Abd al-Malik had it provided with a spacious ambulatory for pilgrims. The design of a circular interior encased in an octagonal exterior and surmounted by a dome is Byzantine. Whereas the beautiful tiles of the exterior were installed by the sixteenth-century Ottoman emperor, Suleiman the Magnificent, the mosaics of the interior date from the building's construction. The motifs of the mosaics are the vases and acanthus leaves so commonly employed in the art of classical antiquity, giant flowers from Persia, and crowns and other ceremonial jewelry in the Byzantine or Persian style. Richard Ettinghausen, an art historian, suggests that the "underlying intent of the decoration seems to have been not only to dazzle the viewer, but even more to proclaim the victory of the final form of divine revelation, and possibly also to demonstrate its world-wide dominion."[1] Perhaps Abd al-Malik was particulary interested in eclipsing the Church of the Holy Sepulchre nearby.

[1] Richard Ettinghausen, *Arab Painting* (Skira, 1961), p. 22.

The Dome of the Rock dominates the Haram ash-Sherif ("the noble sanctuary"), an artificial stone platform thirty-four acres in area and in all probability erected by Herod at the time of the construction of the Second Temple. The Haram ash-Sherif is also the site of the mosque called al-Aqsa ("further" or "furthest") after the opening verses of Sura 17 of the Koran:

> Glory be to Him, who carried His servant by night
> from the Holy Mosque to the Further Mosque
> the precints of which We have blessed,
> that We might show him some of Our signs.[2]

Erected in the early 700s and subsequently rebuilt several times, the mosque is patterned on a Roman Christian basilica but widened to accommodate throngs of worshipers. It has no dome, and its roof is supported by a forest of columns—a characteristic of other large medieval mosques, including those at Cordova and at Qairouan in Tunisia, and al-Azhar in Cairo.

In Damascus the site of the Great Mosque was previously occupied by the Roman Temple of Jupiter and a cathedral containing the tomb of John the Baptist. The Muslims incorporated the tomb into a basilicalike prayer hall more than 400 feet long; adjoining it they placed a huge courtyard, enclosed by a lofty arcade, with columns and capitals in the Roman manner. Expert Byzantine craftsmen installed in the arcade superb mosaics, which show many resemblances to earlier cruder work at Pompeii, Antioch, and Constantinople. Although most of the mosaics were lost in the fires that ravaged the mosque over the centuries, a few have survived, depicting palaces, villas, and peasant cottages along a river, presumably the Barada, which brings water to the Damascus oasis from the Anti-Lebanon mountains. Although the motifs here differ from those encountered in the Dome of the Rock, the intentions seem to have been similar: the Umayyad caliphs were boasting of their success in fixing their capital in the city that claimed to be the oldest in the world.

The Islamic Style

The splendid Umayyad monuments in Jerusalem and Damascus forecast many features of the Islamic artistic style. Architecture continued to be "queen of the arts" with its handmaidens providing the mosaics and tiles, the carvings, lamps, and rugs, the fountains and gardens to embellish the work of the architects. This kind of collaboration produced the Taj Mahal, constructed by a seventeenth-century Muslim ruler at Agra, India, as the tomb for his wife. The jewellike quality of its decoration and the elaborate gardens surrounding it endow this large structure with great delicacy, as if it were as unearthly as something in a fairy tale. E. J. Grube, curator of the Islamic department of the Metropolitan Museum of Art in New York, advances the suggestive idea that Muslim builders aimed at a kind of dematerialization:

> The experience of the infinite on the one hand, with the worthlessness of the transient earthly existence of man on the other is known to all Muslims and forms part of all Muslim art. It finds different but basically related expressions. The most fundamental is the creation of the infinite pattern. . . . The infinite continuation of a given pattern, whether abstract . . . or . . . partly figurative, is on the one hand the expression of a profound belief in the eternity of all true being and on the other a disregard for temporary existence. In making visible only part of a pattern that exists in its complete form only in infinity, the Islamic artist relates the static, limited, seemingly definite object to infinity itself. . . .
>
> One of the most fundamental principles of the

Islamic style deriving from the same basic idea is the dissolution of matter. . . . The ornamentation of surfaces of any kind in any medium with the infinite pattern serves the same purpose—to disguise and "dissolve" the matter, whether it be monumental architecture or a small metal box. . . .

This idea is emphasized by the way in which architectural decoration is used. Solid walls are disguised behind plaster and tile decoration, vaults and arches are covered with floral and epigraphic ornaments that dissolve their structural strength and function, and domes are filled with radiating designs of infinite patterns . . . that banish the solidity of stone and masonry and give them a peculiarly ephemeral quality.[3]

An excellent case in point, besides the Taj Mahal, is the Alhambra, the exquisite, almost unreal palace built at Granada in the twilight of Moorish Spain.

Some of the loveliest Muslim buildings could also serve quite practical purposes. A large mosque was frequently surrounded by satellite structures for schools, hostels, or hospitals. A striking example is the Syrian Military Museum in Damascus, housed in the courtyard of an elegant Ottoman mosque whose outbuildings provided sleeping quarters for pilgrims embarking on the hajj. Muslim rulers liked their palaces as well as their mosques in the grand manner. The palaces ranged from the large villas on the Roman pattern built by the Umayyad caliphs on the fringes of the Syrian desert, to the immense Topkapi complex of the Ottoman emperors in Istanbul. The multitude of relatively small pavilions and kiosks in Topkapi and the spacious gardens and promenades gave it a parklike elegance of scale. The kitchens at Topkapi, ten in all, high-ceilinged and beautifully proportioned, now display the imperial collection of porcelains.

Another example of attention to planning is the city

[3] E. J. Grube, *The World of Islam* (McGraw-Hill, 1966), p. 11.

of Isfahan, capital of Iran under the Safavid dynasty. Shah Abbas (1587–1629) rebuilt it around a great rectangular *maidan*, about one-third of a mile long, which was also his polo field. At one end he placed the vaulted entrance to the Shah's Mosque and at the opposite end the vaulted entrance to the bazaar; all around the maidan were one-story workshops, with a decorative screen of vaulted arches serving as a false second story. The long line of arches, each identical with all the others, exemplifies the almost infinite continuation of pattern noted by Grube. Shah Abbas also made a wide avenue two miles long through the city, with a tree-shaded promenade in the middle, the inspiration, so the story goes, for the Parisian Champs Elysées.

Some Muslim architecture was intimidating as well as handsome, such as the hilltop citadels built at Cairo and at Aleppo by Saladin and his successors about 1200, or the Red Fort of the Mogul emperors of India at Agra (1610). The Seljuk Turks fashioned a remarkable hybrid of military and commercial architecture in the elaborate, fortified *hans* or caravanseries, which they placed every 19 miles or so—a day's caravan journey—along the main routes in Anatolia and Iran. The *hans* and the many bridges, with their graceful pointed arches, erected by the Seljuks and others, indicate that Muslim rulers could outdo the emperors of Rome and ancient Persia in zeal for assuring communications.

Mosques and Their Decoration

The importance of secular architecture notwithstanding, the mosque remains the Islamic work of art par excellence. Though varying widely in style, almost all major mosques have certain common elements that give them a resemblance. Each has its prayer hall, an adjoining courtyard, one or more minarets from which the muezzin sum-

THE ISLAMIC TRADITION

mons the faithful to worship, and a fountain or at least a tap providing running water for ablutions. The first thing a Western visitor notices on entering the prayer hall is likely to be the atmosphere of tranquility and of uncluttered and seemingly unfocused spaciousness. There are no pews or even chairs, no massive furnishings, no compelling central feature like the altar and choir of a church. A second look, however, discloses a focal point in the mihrab, the niche in one wall indicating the direction of Mecca, which has been likened to a miniature version of the Christian apse; although modest in size, it often contains the most beautiful tiles or other decorative work in the mosque. Near the mihrab are the *dikka*, a platform from which an imam can coordinate the prayers of the congregation, and the *minbar*, a pulpit and its staircase of access, from which a sermon may be preached during Friday midday prayers.

The decoration of a mosque avoids painted or carved representations of men and animals as well as of God and the angels. The taboo is based on the following hadith:

> Angels will not enter a house containing a dog or pictures. Aisha relates that she bought a cushion on which were pictures, and when the Apostle of God saw them he stood at the door and would not enter. Seeing signs of displeasure in his face she said: . . . "What have I done amiss?" . . . "Verily," he answered, "the makers of these pictures will be severely punished on the day of resurrection, and it will be said to them, "Bring to life the pictures you have made."[4]

Some scholars believe that the word translated as *pictures* referred only to images of pagan gods, such as the idols removed from the Kaaba; the Prophet, however, may

A. Guillaume, *The Traditions of Islam* (Khayats, 1966), pp. 128–129.

have intended a wider reference, for another hadith reports that he admonished an artist: "If you must needs paint, then paint trees and objects that have not a spirit in them." Historically, the taboo has applied only to embellishment of the Koran and of mosques, tombs, and other religious structures. Persian miniatures illustrated poems and fables with pictures of Muhammad and the angels; the frescoes and mosaics of Umayyad palaces showed hunting scenes, bathing girls, and portraits of Byzantine and Sasanid emperors defeated in battle; and other examples could be cited to show that the taboo was far from absolute, as Westerners sometimes suppose.

In religious decoration craftsmen made the most of the artistic potentialities of leaves, stems, and flowers, and of stars and other geometrical shapes. These are the motifs that helped inspire the tracery of Gothic buildings and brought the word *arabesque* into English to describe flowing, interlacing ornamentation. Above all, Islamic artists raised calligraphy to a fine art. Two main styles of lettering emerged—Kufic (named for the garrison city of Kufa in Iraq), which emphasized angles and vertical lines; and Naskhi (the word means *script*), which was cursive and flowing, often with stress on the horizontal line, and much easier to write than Kufic. To heighten the decorative effect, Naskhi letters might be written one above the other, and Kufic letters might be combined with botanical motives in a "foliated" style or executed so geometrically that a sentence might look like the diagram of a maze. The elaborateness of the medium could make the message undecipherable: Arabs have confessed their inability to read the inscriptions on the Islamic Center in Washington, and a recent study of calligraphy has examples of the *bismillah* ("in the name of God, the merciful, the compassionate") with its letters grotesquely distorted to form the picture of a rooster or a stork.

Regional and Dynastic Variations

The skill of craftsmen, the ingenuity of artists, and the shifting concerns of Muslim dynasties fostered a remarkable number of variations within the general Islamic style. The next few paragraphs offer glimpses of some of the distinctive regional and dynastic substyles. We begin with the Abbasid caliphate.

In Syria and Palestine the Umayyad caliphs had used local stone for their mosques and palaces; in the valleys of Iraq, where stone was unavailable, the Abbasids employed sun-baked bricks, which did not have the permanence of stone. Consequently, nothing is left at Baghdad from the great days of Harun ar-Rashid and Mamun. In the 830s, Mamun's successor transferred the capital to Samarra, 100 miles to the north, where it remained for half a century. The hasty building of an enormous city at Samarra has been described as probably the most ambitious construction project ever attempted by any Muslim dynasty. Among the ruins stretching for miles along the Tigris today, two partially intact structures give some indication both of the gigantic scale of Abbasid Samarra and of its artistic debt to other cultures. One is the triple-arched main gateway to the caliph's palace, which originally covered 400 acres. The deeply-recessed pointed arches show some likeness to the great vaulted hall of the Sasanid emperor's palace at Ctesiphon, near Baghdad, built several centuries earlier; these arches also foreshadow the liwan, a vaulted hall with three walled sides and one open, very frequently encountered in Persian mosques.

The other landmark at Samarra is the massive winding tower, so-called because of the helicoid ramp ascending its exterior, which was the minaret for the largest mosque ever built, equivalent in area to two modern city blocks. The winding tower bears a striking resemblance to reconstructions of ancient Mesopotamian ziggurats, such

as the Tower of Babel. Some idea of what the mosque itself may have been like is suggested by the Mosque of
ibn-Tulun in Cairo, which was built of higher quality brick.
Constructed about A.D. 880 for the Turkish soldier sent
by the Abbasids to govern Egypt, and in part the work of
Iraqi craftsmen, this mosque illustrates the Muslim taste
for endless repetition. It contains well over 100 identical
pointed arches, 128 identical windows (a few still with
their original grilles), and a striking crest motif, rather
like an open keystone, repeated hundreds of times atop its
walls. Inside, there are remnants of the original Kufic
wooden frieze, which was more than a mile long (it en-
circled the structure several times) and reproduced about
one-seventeenth of the Koran. Pottery found at Samarra
demonstrates that Abbasid craftsmen produced cobalt blue
and luster ware and borrowed some of their themes and techniques from the Turks of Central Asia and from the Chinese.

At the opposite end of the Islamic world, meantime,
Muslims in Spain were also turning borrowings to fruit-
ful advantage. The Umayyards, who fled west when the
Abbasids seized the caliphate in A.D. 750, built and re-
peatedly enlarged the great mosque of Cordova until it
became the biggest in Islam outside of Samarra. Its two-
tiered arches were modeled on those of the Roman aque-
ducts in Spain; some arches were made in the horseshoe
shape common in North Africa, and the most elaborate
had cloverleaf scallops cut out of the horseshoe. Especially
in the additions made in the tenth century, the Cordova
mosque has a magnificence contrasting with the austerity
of ibn-Tulun's mosque. In the late 1100s, only a half century before the Christians recaptured Seville, the Muslims
built a mosque with a large, square minaret that now
serves as the bell tower of Seville cathedral. Appropriately,
this Giralda Tower was patterned on a North African
design that ultimately went back to the church towers the
Muslim conquerors had found in Syria. The Giralda Tower

is handsomely decorated with arcaded windows and panels
of intertwining arches.

The ultimate expression of the impulse to transform
stone and plaster into delicate lacework is the Alhambra
of Granada, built in the fourteenth century. Its device of
suspending intricate honeycomb and stalactite designs from
a dome creates the illusion that the ceiling is floating away
like a cloud. Grube seizes on this superb palace as major
evidence confirming his thesis of the Islamic quest for the
dissolution of matter. Other scholars have compared the
Alhambra to an island of tranquility where the king and
his household could retreat from the realities of power
politics engulfing Spanish Muslims.

Seljuks, Safavids, and Ottomans

The most vigorous and inventive Muslim people
artistically were the Seljuk Turks, who began to establish
their reputation as master builders in the eleventh century,
when they were only a generation or two removed from
the pagan, nomadic life of their Central Asian ancestors.
Their art, in turn, continued to develop until it reached
new plateaus of maturity and refinement under the Seljuks'
successors, the Safavid shahs of Persia and the Ottoman
emperors.

From the steppes of Central Asia the Seljuks derived some of the many new elements they introduced
into the Islamic tradition. They wove the first Oriental
rugs, developed from the coverings for tent floors devised
by their pagan forebears as substitutes for animal pelts.
This nomadic Turkish tradition also supplied the abstract
geometrical patterns in the central field of the Seljuk rugs,
whereas the borders used designs based on Kufic Arabic
letters. The nomads' yurt, a circular domed tent of skins
stretched over a lattice frame, very possibly inspired the
characteristic Seljuk tomb, a tower with a conical roof.

The Seljuks introduced also the use of the vaulted liwan in mosque construction, and they were the first to build schools and caravanseries on a grand scale. They experimented with the making of ornamental glazed bricks, discovered new techniques for making tiles in turquoise and cobalt blue, and perfected the inlaying of brass and bronze vessels with intricate patterns of silver.

The major Seljuk structure in Persia is the Friday Mosque in Isfahan, erected by Sultan Malikshah in the late eleventh century. The four large liwan-halls opening from a spacious central courtyard exemplify Seljuk ingenuity in solving technical problems. The vaults of the liwans are strengthened by ribs, a technique later used by Gothic builders in the West; and the transition in the corners from wall to domed roof is facilitated by the device architects call a squinch. Brick is the chief material of the Friday Mosque and is a faded sepia when unglazed, and black, blue, or green when glazed and employed in calligraphic or abstract decorative patterns. The Seljuks applied the same ground plan of courtyard and liwans on a miniature scale for their religious schools.

In Turkey the best specimens of Seljuk architecture are to be found at Konya, capital of the Seljuk Sultanate of Rum. Here, partly because of the harsher Anatolian climate, the schools are enclosed in domed structures, magnificently decorated with colored tiles and bricks. Today these schools are museums, housing an important collection of wood carvings, sculpture, and other Seljuk artifacts. Seljuk edifices in Anatolia often have elaborately carved stone entrance façades and tall brick minarets resembling an ornamental chimney.

Seljuk art exerted a great influence on the two empires that came to rule over its former domains—the Empire of the Safavid Shahs in Iran, and that of the Ottoman Turks farther west. Seljuk forms dominated the monumental structures erected in Isfahan between the

late sixteenth and early eighteenth centuries by Shah
Abbas and his successors. Rows of identical pointed arches,
like those in the walls of the Friday Mosque, constitute
the second-story screen around the great central maidan
and form the spans and parapets of the elegant bridges
crossing the river at the edge of the city. The basic plan
of the Friday Mosque is repeated, with variations, for the
immense Shah's Mosque at the southern end of the maidan
and again for the last major Safavid construction, the
religious school (Mader-i-Shah) flanking Isfahan's Champs
Elysées. Both structures are more exuberant than the
Friday Mosque because of their lavish use of tiles and
mosaics in blue, turquoise, yellow, and white and, in the
Shah's Mosque, because of the loftiness of the main liwan
and the dome above it. The tiled Safavid domes are
among the most beautiful achievements of Islamic art; the
colors of the dome on the religious school seem to match
exactly those in the sky above it, creating once more the
impression that man's handiwork is about to dissolve into
God's. The Persian claim that "half the world is Isfahan"
seems almost modest.

The art of Safavid Persia is more opulent than that
of the Seljuks—some critics would say to an excessive
degree, though a taste for lavish display seems part of the
Persian temperament. Intricate designs in mirror glass
decorated the inner walls of Shah Abbas's "palace of the
forty columns" and fresco portraits of the Shah and his
courtiers the exterior; twenty of the columns were made
of cedars of Lebanon, covered with gold leaf, and twenty
were reflections in the pool in front of the portico. Another
building in the palace compound had inner walls pocketed
with niches in all sorts of shapes. The Persian appetite
for novel effects and variations also affected the design
of rugs. Weavers began to reproduce the dainty miniature
paintings illustrating Persian texts and turned also to large

carpets with intricate floral patterns, sometimes with a
stylized garden, with flowers, trees, and pools.

Gardening has long been regarded as a fine art not
only in Persia but elsewhere in the often arid and treeless
Islamic world. It is reported that when visiting dignitaries
were entertained at a private palace in Beirut a few years
ago, the little pools in the reception room were carpeted
with blossoms in patterns echoing those of the rugs on the
adjoining floor—with the result that an ambassador in-
advertently stepped into one of them. Many of the favorite
flowering plants of the West, including the crocus, tulip,
lilac, and rose, are said to have originated in Persia or its
neighboring countries. The Ottoman Turks supplied Europeans with the tulip bulbs that eventually produced the
speculative "tulipomania" in seventeenth-century Holland.
The Ottomans accorded great respect to skilled gardeners,
and the head gardener at Topkapi Palace was a power in
court politics.

The hyacinth, bluebell, carnation, rose, and, of
course, the tulip were used as motifs on many of the
finest tiles and pottery produced by the Ottomans. Sixteenth-century craftsmen at Iznik (the ancient Nicea)
perfected a new technique of applying a glaze over colors
before a tile was fired. This process enabled them to solve
the perennial problem of obtaining a red that would not
fade by putting on red pigment so thickly that raised
veins may be felt under the glaze of a tile wherever the
color appears. Although the technique is now a lost art,
magnificent examples of Iznik work may be seen in the
tiles adorning some of the buildings in the Topkapi compound and in several of the Istanbul mosques.

Again with the Ottoman Turks, their supreme artistic
achievement was their mosques. They built an astonishing
number of important ones, ranging from early structures
of largely Seljuk design to some adaptations of European

baroque and neoclassical styles made in the empire's declining centuries. The most splendid mosques date from
the sixteenth century and were mainly designed by one
man, Sinan, the talented and prolific chief architect of
Suleiman the Magnificent. Two features, in particular, char-
acterize Ottoman mosques—massive domes, and tall, slender
minarets, which are very elegant and also need frequent
rebuilding. The Ottomans transformed the Seljuk liwans
into spacious domed chambers; to enlarge the area of
ceiling that could be supported without interior columns,
Sinan used auxiliary half-domes flanking the main dome,
a Byzantine device applied so successfully many centuries
earlier when Santa Sophia was built. At first glance, consequently, in external appearance the great sixteenth-
century mosques of Istanbul all look like first cousins of
Justinian's great church. Their handsome stone exteriors,
beautifully proportioned but largely undecorated, make the
Seljuk façades look almost fussy by contrast and the
mosques of Safavid Persia downright gaudy. The interior
of the great Ottoman mosque, with its delicate Iznik tiles,
with its enormous volume of enclosed space unbroken by
intruding columns, and with a sheik and a few acolytes
in some corner softly reciting the Koran, expresses very
well the Islamic concept of the world of prayer as a
counterpoint to the workaday world.

Prose Literature

No work of art, not even the mosque, holds a position in the Islamic tradition comparable to that of the
Koran in literature. In fact if literature is defined as a
human creation, the Koran cannot be judged by literary
standards alone, since it is the speech of God. And yet,
as Philip K. Hitti observes:

> The inimitability associated with the book did not arrest
> its lasting, incalculable literary influence on subsequent

THE ARTS AND LITERATURE

Arabic output. The effect of the King James translation of the Bible on English is slight compared to the effect of the Koran on Arabic. It was the Koran that kept the unity of the language and prevented its fragmentation into dialect.[5]

Technically, the Koran is prose, though it has some of the rhyming and rhythmic qualities of poetry. Earlier chapters of this book have introduced other characteristic forms of Islamic prose, including the hadiths, the lives of Sufi saints, the autobiographies of al-Ghazali and Avicenna, and the religious, philosophical, and scientific writings of Muslim intellectuals in general.

Ask a Westerner to name one work of Islamic prose, however, and he will probably ignore all those already mentioned and choose *The Arabian Nights*. The stories in *The Thousand and One Nights* (to translate its Arabic title) are far from purely Arab but an amalgam built up over several centuries. As Professor Hitti notes, "Their heterogeneous character inspired the modern critical remark that *The Arabian Nights* are Persian tales told after the manner of Buddha by Queen Esther to Harun al-Rashid in Cairo during the fourteenth Christian century."[6] Muslims rank the literary distinction of these tales much below that of an earlier work in a similar vein—*Kalila and Dimna,* an eighth-century Arabic translation from the Persian of Sanskrit fables recounted by two jackals. Here is one of them. Dimna informs Kalila:

> "You know how it is, a treacherous attack launched from an unexpected quarter is always the most successful. That's how the hare destroyed the lion, you remember."
> "No, I can't say I do," Kalila said. So Dimna told him.
> In a certain meadow, which the soft breeze per-

[5] Philip K. Hitti, *Islam: A Way of Life* (University of Minnesota Press, 1970), p. 151.
[6] Hitti, *Islam: A Way of Life,* p. 154.

fumed with the sweet odour of Paradise, and the re-
flection of its sheen brightened the countenance of
Heaven, where a thousand stars glittered on every branch
and a thousand spheres stared amazed at every star,
many beasts came to graze and water and to enjoy the
lush plenty there abounding. But in the neighbourhood
there was a lion, which quite spoiled the ease and com-
fort of the other animals. So one day they . . . decided
to speak to the lion.

"Look," they said. "Every day after much toil
and boundless hardship you succeed in catching and
chewing up just one of us. We are always in a frightful
flap, and you have all the bother of searching. Now
we've thought up a scheme whereby you can be free
of trouble and worry, and we can live quietly and at
ease. If you agree to stop chasing us, every day without
fail we will send one of our number at dinner-time. . . ."

The lion consented to this arrangement, and
matters so continued for some time. Then one day the
lot fell upon the hare.

"My friends," he addressed his fellow animals,
"if you are willing to be a little indulgent about sending
me, I guarantee to rescue you all from this bloodthirsty
tyrant."

"Well, there's no harm in trying," they agreed.

So he delayed for an hour or so, until the lion's
dinnertime was past; then he shuffled off slowly in his
direction. He spied the lion looking very upset; the fires
of hunger blazed within his belly, fanned by the wind
of emptiness. . . . When he saw the hare coming, he
let out a great roar.

"They sent another hare along with me," the hare
explained. "But on the way a lion seized him. I told him
over and over again that he was the king's meal, but he
took no notice. As a matter of fact he was very rude
about you. He said this was his hunting-ground, and
anyway the hare belonged to him by right because he
was stronger than you. So I hurried on to tell your
majesty."

"Show me where he is!" the lion roared. . . .

The hare . . . brought the lion in no time to a
well of sparkling water, bright and clear as a mirror,

THE ARTS AND LITERATURE

so that every face and form was reflected in it in all its
details. . . .

"He's in this well," the hare whispered. "I'm
afraid of him. But if the king will take me into his bosom
I will show him his enemy."

The lion picked up the hare, and peeped into
the well. Seeing the image of himself and the hare, he at
once dropped the hare and flung himself into the well
and was drowned. So the hare came back safe and
sound to the other animals, who all crowded round and
asked him what had happened.

"Oh, I drowned the lion," the hare said modestly.[7]

Although this engaging fable has much more in common
with Aesop than with Islam, the writing has the flowery
eloquence often encountered in Islamic prose.

But there is also a large body of more informal
Islamic folk literature, which has experienced a revival of
popularity in the past century because it contains so much
native nationalist wisdom to set against Western colonialist
culture. A proverb can deliver a real sting in a few words:

Among walnuts only the empty one speaks.
He who has money can eat sherbet in hell.
We traded in shrouds; people stopped dying.
His brains hang at the top of his fez.
Walls have mice and mice have ears.
Trust in God, but tie your camel.
He gives a party with bath-water.
A camel can die of thirst carrying water on his back.[8]

Poetry

Just as some proverbs can be traced back to pre-
Islamic days, the themes and traditions of Arabic poetry
go back to the *qasida*, the Bedouin ode of the century in

[7] Arberry, *Aspects of Islamic Civilization*, pp. 92–93.
[8] All but the last are quoted in James Kritzeck, *Anthology of
Islamic Literature* (Holt, Rinehart & Winston, 1964), pp. 64–65.

which Muhammad was born. Later, the introductory section of the qasida, in which the memories of a past love engulfed the poet, became an independent lyric, the *ghazal*. The ghazal treated the classic themes of romantic love— the passion or sorrow of the lover, the indifference or faithlessness of his beloved, and the skepticism of the old hand at the game. Some scholars believe that the ghazals of Muslim Spain served as models for the poems of courtly love sung by the Christian troubadours further north in the developing Romance vernaculars. Others, however, argue that both the Romance and Arabic poets looked back to older Mediterranean poetic traditions. In any case, we know that poets in Muslim Spain were fluent in both Arabic and Romance, and that both were sometimes used in the same poem, an intricate form of ghazal called the *muwashshah* ("girdled").

In the following *muwashshah* the "girdle" consists of the lines ending in *-aim (-ame)* and *-ess*. The fact that at the very end the style shifts from high-flown to slangy, and the language from Arabic to Romance, suggests that the poet may have borrowed from popular ditties in the vernacular sung by itinerant entertainers.

My heaving sighs proclaim   Love's joys are bitterness
        My heart has lost her mentor,
        She spurns my anguished cry
        And craves for her tormentor;
        If I hide love, I die.
When 'Oh heart!' I exclaim   My foes mock my distress.
        O tearful one who chantest
        Of mouldering ditch and line,
        Or hopefully decantest,
        I have no eyes for thine.
Let yearning glow aflame,   Tears pour in vain excess.
        Mine eye, love's tribute venting,
        Expended all its store,
        Then its own pain lamenting
        Began to weep once more.

My heart is past reclaim   Or sweet forgetfulness.
                    I blame it not for weeping
                    My heart's distress to share,
                    As, weary but unsleeping,
                    It probed the starry sphere.
To count them was my aim   But they are numberless.
                    A doe there was I trysted
                    (No lion is as tough).
                    I came, but she insisted
                    'Tomorrow', and sheered off.
Hey, folks, d'you know that game?   And what's the gal's address?[9]

The ghazal and the *muwashshah* could serve as more than a showcase for a poet's cleverness and conceits. The Sufis employed them to express in symbolic terms their love of God, for which their favored metaphors were wine and earthly love. Here is part of a ghazal by Jalal ud-din Rumi, famous both as a poet and as founder of the Mevlevi dervishes:

Come Saki, hand me a cup of dark wine
    that in the Magian cloister I may perceive Reality.
Remorse I've cast aside, that in full contenment
    for a time I may sit happily at the tavern door.
I care nought for penitence, self-denial, or piety,
    now that I find my happiness there.
I'll throw off cant, pretense, and sanctimony
    and let the vat-house Saki draw deep draughts for me.
And when I drain the life-restoring cup he hands me,
    I'll shift the garb of abstinence and devotion from the cloister.
Come then, my beloved, leave your secluded chamber,
    that in your face my woeful heart may find its joy.
'Tis towards it that men of insight turn in their devotions;
    and should I divert my cheek, then have I lost my faith.[10]

The ambiguous quality of such poems makes them difficult to interpret; one is never quite sure to what extent they

    [9] Quoted by H. A. R. Gibb, *Arabic Literature*, 2nd ed. (Clarendon Press, 1963), pp. 111–112.
    [10] Reuben Levy, *An Introduction to Persian Literature* (Columbia University Press, 1969), p. 103.

should be read literally and to what extent symbolically.

Jalal ud-din Rumi was a Persian, one of the "great choir of poets" whose culture, in Emerson's judgment, "perpetually reinforced through 500 years, again and again has enabled the Persians to refine and civilize their conquerors and to preserve their national identity." No country in the world venerates its poets more. Their names—Firdausi, Sa'di, Hafiz—are borne by the chief avenues in Tehran, and their tombs are patriotic shrines. While they are national heroes, they are not necessarily Islamic heroes, for it is often claimed that some of them used the veiled language of the Sufi to defend skeptical, materialistic, or hedonistic views very hard to reconcile with Islam.

A case in point is the mathematician-astronomer-poet, Omar Khayyam, who died in 1123 and is credited with perfecting a new verse form, the *rubai* (from the Arabic for *four*), or quatrain, in which all lines rhyme except the third, which affords a breathing spell before the final line. In 1858 Edward Fitzgerald translated some of Omar's quatrains in the famous *Rubaiyat*. He asked his readers to agree that, for example, when Omar talked about wine, he meant "simply the juice of the grape," not something transcendental. Accordingly, Omar was read literally and acquired a reputation as a champion of high living and as a rationalist, cynic, and pessimist.

Recently, however, a Persian scholar, Omar Ali-Shah, and an English poet, Robert Graves, have published a new translation from a manuscript claimed to be both older and more authentic than that used by Fitzgerald. They argue vigorously that Omar was a Sufi and put great store on the fact that, like his contemporary al-Ghazali, he quit a successful professorship in midcareer to cultivate the Sufi pathway. Two key quatrains are printed below; in each case the Fitzgerald version is followed by the newer one. After reading them, one may not feel competent to judge which is closer to the spirit of

the original, but one gains fresh appreciation of how
hazardous it is to clarify the Islamic image cast by entities
as protean as poetry and Sufism.

> Alike for those who for TO-DAY prepare,
> And those that after a TO-MORROW stare,
>   A Muezzin from the Tower of Darkness cries:
> "Fools! your Reward is neither Here nor There!"[11]

> Some ponder long on doctrine and belief,
> Some teeter between certitude and doubt.
> Suddenly out of hiding leaps the Guide
> With: "Fools, the Way is neither that nor this."[12]

> Ah, make the most of what we yet may spend,
> Before we too into the Dust descend:
>   Dust into Dust, and under Dust, to lie,
> Sans Wine, sans Song, sans Singer, and—sans End![13]

> Most of them, gone before we go, my Saki,
> Drowse in their dusty bed of pride, my Saki.
> Drink yet again and hear the truth at last:
> "Whatever words they spoke were wind, my Saki."[14]

[11] Edward Fitzgerald, *Rubaiyat of Omar Khayyam,* fourth
edition, Quatrain XXV, in *Works of Edward Fitzgerald* (Houghton,
Mifflin, 1887), I, p. 33.
[12] Robert Graves and Omar Ali-Shah, *The Original Rubaiyyat
of Omar Khayaam* (Doubleday, 1968), p. 55. Permission by Collins-
Knowlton-Wing, Inc.
[13] Fitzgerald, *op. cit.,* Quatrain XXIV, p. 31.
[14] Graves and Ali-Shah, p. 55.

THE MODERN
CHALLENGE

The Islamic tradition—in thought and culture as well as in religion—is almost wholly a product of the Middle Ages. During the five centuries since the Ottoman Turks took Byzantium in 1453 little new has been added to it, and much that was central to medieval Islam has been threatened by the pervasive challenge of modern Western civilization. In Southeast Asia and Indonesia, on the Indian subcontinent, and in North Africa Muslim states passed under some form of Western colonial rule. The Persian and Ottoman empires, which were Muslim strongholds in the sixteenth and seventeenth centuries, remained independent in name but suffered serious erosion of their territories and sovereignty as a result of repeated European intervention in their affairs. The scientific and industrial revolutions gave the West such a head start that all the non-Western peoples seemed destined to remain junior partners in a world enterprise dominated by the great powers of Europe and North America.

The Muslim Peoples Today

One could sketch an image of modern Islam as the helpless victim of historical forces beyond its control, clinging to traditional patterns of thought and action as the only way of dealing with a challenge it could not meet directly. Such an image would be a gross simplification and distortion of realities. The Muslim peoples have not proved to be uniformly helpless and have played their full part in the great revolution against colonialism that gained momentum from World War I and has radically redrawn the political map of the world since World War II. Turkey, Iran, and Egypt cast off the last vestiges of colonial tutelage and became independent in fact as well as in name. Since 1945 an impressively long list of Muslim states have gained independence: Indonesia, Malaysia, Pakistan, Iraq, Syria, Jordan, Libya, Tunisia, Algeria, and Morocco, to name only the most important. The roll call can go on through Kuwait and the other former British protectorates in the Arabian peninsula, and through the band of African states stretching across the continent at its widest point, from Mauritania and Senegal on the Atlantic to Somalia on the Indian Ocean.

The total Muslim population of the world in 1971 was estimated to be somewhere between 500 million and 700 million; this means broadly that one person out of every six in the world is Muslim. The largest Muslim community is that of the Indian subcontinent, totaling about 150 million. Almost as large is the community in the Middle East, including Turkey, Iran (now the official name for Persia), and Afghanistan as well as the Arab world. Next come Southeast Asia and Indonesia, with more than 100 million. North Africa has 35 million, and the rest of the continent at least 50 million, though reliable statistics are lacking. Estimates of the Muslim population in communist China range all the way from 12 million to 50 million, the uncertainty arising in part because many Muslims are believed to have fled from Sinkiang, the western province of China, to adjacent areas of the Soviet Union. Aside from these refugees, the Soviet Muslims number about 25 million; they are mainly Turkic peoples living in the large area of Central Asia that used to be called Turkestan and also in parts of the Caucasus and along the middle Volga.

Nationalism and Communism

Among the important forces underlying these statistics is the growing self-awareness, the mounting nationalism of Muslim peoples. The 1947 partition of the Indian subcontinent into the Islamic Republic of Pakistan and the Republic of India represented the conviction of Muslims that because the Hindus had not learned to live with them, the two faiths had better live separately. At least one-third of the Muslims in the subcontinent continue to live in the Republic of India, however. In the Soviet Union, where it was once supposed that Islam was due for extinction because of communism's antireligious militance, the Muslim peoples have managed to work within the communist system and also to resist assimilation by the numerically and politically preponderant Russians. While only the old cling to traditional Muslim ways, both young and old are emerging from their traditional isolation to make contact with other Islamic peoples and to realize that Muslims have fared better in the Soviet Union than in neighboring China.

In Indonesia, during the early years of independence, some Muslims seem to have accepted the argument that Muhammad and Marx preached compatible social and economic doctrines. Yet in 1965 when President Sukarno's erratic fellow-traveling regime permitted communist conspirators to plot a political takeover, Muslim officers foiled the plot and Muslim students took the lead in the subsequent massacres, which are thought to have taken the lives of perhaps 300,000 alleged communists and fellow travelers. Clearly, there is some justification for the West's confidence that Islam is a bulwark against communism, but it is also clear that Muslims, too, can be pragmatists and enlist communist support when it seems to be in their best interest. Witness the attitudes of Muslims in the USSR, and witness, too, the military alliances made with the Soviets by Algeria and Egypt.

Black Africa

Perhaps the most persuasive evidence of the vitality of modern Islam is that it continues to be a missionary religion exhibiting much more dynamism than an image of reactionary traditionalism would suggest. The ranks of Muslim converts are swelling in the lands on the western and southern fringes of the band of Muslim states spanning sub-Saharan Africa—in Guinea, Sierra Leone, parts of Liberia and Nigeria, southern Sudan, and perhaps also in the old Christian bastion of Ethiopia. A recent informed source estimates that at least one African out of three is a Muslim and that for every African converted to Christianity nine or ten become Muslims.[1]

The margin of success enjoyed by Islam in Black Africa no doubt comes in part because Islam does not bear the Christian white man's burden of identification with racism and imperialism. Yet here again we must not oversimplify, for in parts of East Africa Islamic missions have suffered reverses because so many of the Muslims already on the scene have been Arab and Indian immigrants who have virtually monopolized the roles of merchant and shopkeeper. Moreover, orthodox Muslims are often horrified at the readiness of Islamic missionaries to make concessions to tribal customs and prejudices. The converts may continue recourse to charms, amulets, and magic belts and venerate almost any local dignitary who claims to be a mahdi or to have saintly qualities. Here is

[1] J. Kritzeck and W. H. Lewis, *Islam in Africa* (Van Nostrand Reinhold, 1969), p. 2.

a situation imperiling orthodoxy, comparable to the cult of the marabout in Morocco or the entry of so many Hindu elements into Indian sufism.

The Inner Crisis and the Wahabi Response

Most scholars agree, however, that the greatest crisis faced by modern Islam has come not from external threats but from within. Politically and militarily, its symbol in the eighteenth and nineteenth centuries was the reputation of the Ottoman Empire as the "sick man of Europe," doomed to succumb in any struggle where the fittest would survive. Economically, the Ottoman Turks appeared too proud to compete; and they let commercial domination of their empire pass almost by default into the eager hands of its non-Muslim minorities—Greeks, Armenians, Copts, Jews—and their European partners. Religiously, the creative energies of the Islamic world seemed to have dried up toward the close of the Middle Ages. The Asharite theology and the Sharia continued to prevail in an increasingly rigid and stultified way, and the ulema came more often to be criticized for obscurantism than praised for their learning. It was scarcely surprising that some Muslims accepted some adulteration of Islam by the more vital practices and beliefs of others.

The adulteration went too far and aroused a fundamentalist reaction that has proved to be one of the characteristic responses to the inner crisis of Islam and to the whole modern challenge. The reaction began in the eighteenth century with the emergence of the Wahabi movement in the Arabian peninsula. Muhammad ibn Abd al-Wahab ("son of the slave of the Bestower," the reference is to one of the ninety-nine names of God) was a Sufi who became convinced that the popular practice of Sufism with its preoccupation with saints and sheiks was leading men into what the Prophet called the deadliest sin, the assigning of partners to God. Calling themselves *unitarians,* the Wahabis preached a strict monotheism and stripped Islamic practice of what they felt to be unnecessary trappings; they prayed in mosques without minarets, for example, and with gravel rather than rugs on the floor. They revived the most conservative pathway of the law, the Hanbali, which had fallen into desuetude, and, finding the consensus on major religious issues reached by the ulema in the ninth and tenth centuries too lax and permissive, they insisted on returning to the customs and beliefs prevailing under Muhammad himself. In their militancy and puritanism they were not unlike the Kharijites of Islam or the early Protestants of Christianity with their appeals for literal interpretation of Scripture and a return to the primitive Church.

The Wahabis early entered a political alliance with the Saudi family. From their capital at Riyadh in the center of Arabia, the Saudis conquered Mecca and most of the peninsula in the early nineteenth century, only to lose their conquests to the Ottoman Empire, when the emperor commissioned his powerful Egyptian vassal, Muhammad Ali, to recover the lands of the lucrative pilgrim trade. The Saudis reemerged from obscurity at the beginning of the twentieth century under Abdul Aziz ibn-Saud, who gradually brought most of the peninsula under his control, created the Kingdom of Saudi Arabia, and licensed Aramco (the Arabian-American Oil Company) to exploit its oil. The new wealth did little to change ibn-Saud's traditional Bedouin ways or devotion to Wahabism; and his kingdom was identified in world opinion with the strict seclusion of women, hostility to such modern inventions as the motion picture, television, and the cocktail, and enforcement of penalties traditionally prescribed, like severing the hand of a convicted thief. Although some relaxation of Saudi policies has occurred since the death of ibn-Saud in 1953, the kingdom remains a stronghold of Muslim conservatism.

The Muslim Brotherhood

In the twentieth century movements somewhat similar to Wahabism have appeared in several Muslim countries. In Pakistan the Jamaat-i-Islam ("community of Islam") stood for vesting supreme political authority in the ulema; in Iran the Fadayan Islam ("devotees of Islam") specialized in attempts on the lives of political leaders identified with secular, pro-Western interests. And in Egypt the Muslim Brotherhood, which will serve as our case history of these movements, aroused wide concern among Westerners because it copied the paramilitary organizations and some of the other techniques of European totalitarianism. Much more was involved in the Muslim Brotherhood, however, than transplanted fascism. Claiming that "Allah is our legislator, the Koran our constitution," it formulated a program for restoring the caliphate and purging the Egyptian monarchy of its liberal constitution (modeled on that of Belgium) and all its other Western paraphernalia. Its founder was a young schoolteacher, Hasan al-Banna, who had also been trained in the Hanbali school of law and had had some experience with a Sufi brotherhood and with Muslim counterparts of the YMCA. He was well equipped to fuse orthodoxy, the popular Sufi tradition, and a twentieth-century concern for social problems.

The *Muslim Brethren* (as the organization is often termed) came into being in 1928 at Ismailia, the "company town" of the British garrison guarding the Suez Canal and the European enterprise operating it. Ismailia exemplified the enormous gap between the comfortable standard of living enjoyed by the foreigners and the marginal one of the meagerly paid Egyptians. The Brethren specialized in denouncing the moral poisons being introduced by the Westerners, castigating government officials for dishonoring their families by allowing photographs of their wives and daughters to appear in the press. From the beginning, however, the Brotherhood maintained an ambitious social program, offering free adult education and free medical services, and experimenting with textile and printing cooperatives owned by the men who worked in them.

For these reasons, and also because the monarchy of King Farouk catered to the interests of the wealthy few, the Brotherhood became one of the very few organizations in the modern Muslim world to win a mass following. It appears to have been more successful in penetrating to the grass roots than any of Nasser's later attempts at a single all-inclusive political party. Estimates of the Brotherhood's membership at its peak range from fifty or one hundred thousand all the way to a million and a half or two million, though the higher figures certainly include many sympathizers in addition to participants. The peak coincided with the disastrous Palestinian War of 1948, which exposed the unpreparedness and corruption of Farouk's regime. Government efforts to suppress the Brotherhood led to the assassination of a ranking minister by a Brother and then to the assassination of al-Banna himself in 1949, presumably at the instigation of the government.

Although the Brotherhood never recovered from the loss of its gifted and dedicated leader, it remained an important factor in the hectic politics of the next few years. A clash between Egyptian police and British troops in Ismailia touched off the destructive Black Saturday riot in Cairo (January 26, 1952). The extent of the Brethren's role has never been fully established; but many targets of the rioters were fixtures of the European and upper class Egyptian way of life so deplored by the Brethren—Shepheard's Hotel, the Jockey Club, Groppi's restaurant and catering establishment, the Chemla and Cicurel department stores (the latter owned by the family of Mme. Pierre Mendès-France), the big downtown movie houses, and prominent bars and night clubs. Six months later, a revolution carried out by a small group of discontented young officers swept

away the monarchy and set up the regime that Colonel
Nasser was to head for almost two decades. The Muslim
Brethren soon fell out with the new government because
of its intention of furthering the emancipation of women
and modernizing the theological university of al-Azhar and
the courts of Sharia law.

Pan-Islam and Islamic Modernism

Total rejection of the West was not the only Islamic
response to the modern challenge. Some Muslims argued
that Islam must adopt Western techniques in order to check
and reverse the tide of Western imperialism. One such
technique was to forge the solidarity of Muslim peoples
against the imperialists, to foster the concept of Pan-Islam
on the model of the Pan-German and Pan-Slavic movements in Europe. The first Pan-Islamic propagandist was
Jamal ad-Din al-Afghani (1839–1897), who was active in
Afghanistan, India, Russia, Egypt, the Ottoman Empire,
and, above all, Iran. He had an important part in provok-
ing the successful Persian "tobacco riots" of the early 1890s
against the grant of a lucrative monopoly to the British; and
one of his henchmen subsequently assassinated the shah
who had permitted so many foreign encroachments on
Persian sovereignty. After al-Afghani's death his teachings
helped to inspire the insurgents who staged the Persian
revolution of 1905–1906, which began a long struggle to
transform an ineffectual absolute monarchy into a constitutional regime more capable of defending Iran against
Western imperialism.

On the international scene, however, the Pan-Islamic
idea proved to be an insignificant force. It did convince the
Ottoman emperor, Abdul Hamid II, that he should exploit
the long-neglected potentialities of the title of caliph. He
made a point of giving government posts to Arabs and
members of other non-Turkish Muslim minorities in the

empire; he assisted the resettlement of Muslim refugees from Russian persecution; and he built the Hejaz Railway from Damascus to Medina to facilitate the hajj. Yet when his successor proclaimed a jihad on Turkey's entry into World War I on the side of the Central Powers, the appeal had little impact on the many millions of Muslims under the rule of the Allies.

Al-Afghani also urged Muslims to revitalize their thinking by adopting Western rationalism. Early in his career he delivered a lecture in Istanbul asserting that prophecy and reason were equally valid guides to religious truth. The faithful were scandalized by the implication that the thought of man was on a par with the word of God, and al-Afghani was obliged to leave the Ottoman Empire. His Egyptian disciple, Muhammad Abduh (1845–1905), continued the campaign to convince Muslims that it was both necessary and proper to study Western science and reason in order to defend the faith. He particularly advocated reading two thinkers then considered in the vanguard of materialism—Herbert Spencer, the English social Darwinist, and Auguste Comte, the French positivist. Abduh gained the favor of the British, who had occupied Egypt in 1882; he became the chief judge of a Sharia court and was placed in charge of modernizing the narrowly traditionalist curriculum at al-Azhar, where he had studied in his youth. Though it was not until after the Egyptian revolution of 1952 that a full reform was attempted at al-Azhar, by 1914 more and more Muslims were studying in the West or in Western-style schools and universities at home.

Kemalist Secularism

The Islamic modernism identified with Abduh and his followers sought to preserve the faith; the much more drastic modernism practiced by the Turkish Republic after World War I seemed intent on uprooting Islam. Postwar

Turkey, a geographically shrunken state limited mainly to Anatolia, had lost the large Christian minorities of Ottoman days so that its population was now 99 percent Muslim. Kemal Atatürk, the founder of the republic, argued that it could survive and prosper only if it gave up the bad old customs of the Ottoman Empire. The sweeping reforms made by Atatürk in the 1920s and 1930s were a wholesale repudiation of the Islamic tradition. The republic abolished the caliphate and declared secularism one of the guiding principles of its constitution. New law codes based on advanced Western models, were introduced and the Sharia scrapped as totally incompatible with progress. The republic banned religious instruction in state schools and required civil marriage ceremonies. It forbade the building of new mosques, discouraged the repair of old ones, dissolved the surviving dervish brotherhoods, prohibited the wearing of distinctive clerical garb, and banned the use of Arabic in the call to prayer.

The Kemalist revolution upset many of the details of everyday life. It forbade the brimless fez, considering it to be a symbol of Ottoman backwardness, and directed men to wear hats in the Western style, so much less well adapted to use in the prostrations of prayer. Though even Atatürk did not venture to ban the wearing of the veil, he discouraged its use and sponsored measures giving women full legal equality with men. Perhaps the most radical innovation of all was the Kemalist jettisoning of the Arabic script in which Ottoman Turkish had been written and the substitution of a new Latin alphabet much better suited to the phonetic spelling of the language, which is rich in vowels, and considerably easier for students to master.

By the time of Atatürk's death in 1938 the Turkish rank and file had come to accept or at least tolerate many features of the Kemalist program, but not all. The conservative eastern provinces simply ignored the requirement for civil marriage ceremonies, as an example. The fact that secularism deeply wounded Muslim sensibilities contributed to the defeat suffered by Atatürk's old party in the Turkish Republic's first free election in 1950. The victorious Democrats soon restored religious education in state schools, permitted the building and renovation of mosques, allowed the call to prayer in Arabic once again, and winked at dervish activity. Although subsequent Turkish governments have maintained these concessions, they have refused to yield on issues involving the legal system or the alphabet.

The kind of situation prevailing in Turkey exists to some degree in other Muslim countries. Wherever governments are seeking a more effective and responsive legal and judicial apparatus, the Sharia is being eroded. Yet there is also much evidence of widespread personal participation in the activities of the faith, and not just among the traditionalist peasants. A recent survey notes the recognition of sixty-four dervish brotherhoods in Egypt, and Sufi retreats attract Western-educated men of the upper middle class. At the American University of Beirut, one of the most thoroughly Westernized educational centers in the Middle East, Muslim students are reported to observe the fast of Ramadan for only part of each week, for as long as they can without impairing their academic efficiency. To risk a sweeping generalization: on the popular level, as contrasted with the institutional level, the Islamic tradition appears strong. But on the level of the Sharia and the ulema, who have historically provided the guidance and discipline to check the excesses of popular religion, the Islamic tradition has not so far been able to respond successfully to the modern challenge and may succumb elsewhere, as it already seems to have done in Turkey.

BIBLIOGRAPHY

(Note: In each section below, standard authorities and the most useful references are listed first, followed by more specialized works and other important titles.)

REFERENCE WORKS

The Encyclopaedia of Islam, 4 vols. (Brill, 1913–1938).
This is the indispensable corpus of scholarly articles with full bibliographies. It is rather baffling to the beginner, because many entries are listed under the initial of a name or title in Arabic. "Avicenna" will be found as Ibn Sina, for example, and the "Muslim Brotherhood" under *"Ikhwan."*

Publication of a much-revised second edition began in the 1950s and, as of 1971, had proceeded through the middle of the entries under the letter *I;* articles from the first edition on religion and law were revised and reprinted as *The Shorter Encyclopaedia of Islam* (1953).

CAHEN, CLAUDE (ed.). *Jean Sauvaget's Introduction to the History of the Muslim East: A Bibliographical Guide* (University of California, 1965). Translation of a French work, with useful comments on the titles listed.

HOLT, P. M., LAMBTON, ANN K. S., and LEWIS, BERNARD (eds.). *The Cambridge History of Islam* (Cambridge University Press, 1970). Two hefty volumes of scholarly articles; the first volume treats the central Islamic lands, the second the further Islamic lands and Islamic civilization.

ARBERRY, A. J. (ed.). *Religion in the Middle East* (Cambridge University Press, 1969). Volume II deals with Islam, mainly on the basis of a country-by-country survey.

RONART, S., and RONART, N. *Concise Encyclopaedia of Arabic Civilization* (Praeger, 1960, 1966). Volume I treats the Arab east, volume II the Arab west.

SPULER, B. *The Muslim World: A Historical Survey,* 3 vols.

(Brill, 1960–1969). Translation of a manual by a German scholar; emphasizes political history.

ARNOLD, T., and GUILLAUME, A. (eds.). *The Legacy of Islam* (Oxford University Press, 1931), and A. J. ARBERRY (ed.). *The Legacy of Persia* (Clarendon, 1953). Essays by leading scholars, chiefly on artistic, literary, and intellectual topics.

HAZARD, H. W. *Atlas of Islamic History*, 2nd ed. (Princeton University Press, 1952). Maps and tables illustrating the expansion and contraction of Islamic lands century by century. R. Roolvink, *Historical Atlas of the Muslim Peoples* (Harvard University Press, 1958) should also be consulted.

GENERAL STUDIES

GIBB, H. A. R. *Mohammedanism*, 2nd ed. (Oxford University Press, 1953). Masterly brief introduction by a scholar of the first rank. May be supplemented by *Studies on the Civilization of Islam* (Beacon, 1962), a collection of Gibb's articles, two of which are of wide scope and interest: "An Interpretation of Islamic History" and "The Structure of Religious Thought in Islam."

VON GRUNEBAUM, G. E. *Classical Islam* (Aldine, 1970). A history down to the Mongol conquest of Baghdad, 1258, with useful chronological tables and an excellent critical bibliography. May be supplemented by the same scholar's sometimes controversial interpretative articles collected in *Islam* (Routledge & Kegan Paul, 1955) and *Medieval Islam*, 2nd ed. (Phoenix, 1953).

RAHMAN, FAZLUR. *Islam* (Anchor, 1966). Comprehensive introduction by a Pakistani scholar; valuable for giving a Muslim's insights into his faith.

GOITEIN, S. D. *Studies in Islamic History and Institutions* (Brill, 1966). Important scholarly articles on the nature of Islam and the details of its religious, political, and social institutions.

HITTI, P. K. *Islam: A Way of Life* (University of Minnesota Press, 1970). Brief enlightening lectures on the Islamic state and Islamic culture as well as the faith itself by a scholar of Lebanese Christian background. See also Hitti's *A History of the Arabs*, 10th ed. (St. Martin's, 1970).

SAUNDERS, J. J. *A History of Medieval Islam* (Barnes & Noble, 1965). Clear and up-to-date.

BROCKELMANN, C. *A History of the Islamic Peoples* (Capricorn, 1947). An older work stressing political narrative.

LEWIS, BERNARD. *The Arabs in History* (Torchbooks, 1950). Lively and informative brief survey.

GUILLAUME, A. *Islam* (Penguin, 1954). Informative introduction by an able scholar.

GOLDZIHER, I. *Muslim Studies*, 2 vols. (Allen & Unwin, 1967, 1970). Translations of essays first published nearly a century ago and still worth reading as foundations of modern Islamic scholarship.

SCHUON, FRITHJOF. *Understanding Islam* (Allen & Unwin, 1963). Sympathetic interpretation from a mystical point of view; assumes the reader is already acquainted with the basics of the faith.

ANTHOLOGIES

KRITZECK, J. *Anthology of Islamic Literature* (Holt, Rinehart & Winston, 1964). Well-chosen selections covering the full range of the subject.

JEFFERY, A. *A Reader on Islam* (Mouton, 1962). Passages from standard Arabic writings illustrating the beliefs and practices of Muslims.

ARBERRY, A. J. *Aspects of Islamic Civilization* (Allen and Unwin, 1964). A highly personal selection (all the translations are by Arberry). Not fully representative but including some fascinating items.

WILLIAMS, J. A. (ed.). *Islam* (Braziller, 1961). Another useful compilation of source readings.

WESTERN IMAGES OF ISLAM

SOUTHERN, R. W. *Western Views of Islam in the Middle Ages* (Harvard University Press, 1962). Excellent analysis.

DANIEL, N. A. *Islam and the West: The Making of an Image* and *Islam, Europe and Empire* (Edinburgh University Press, 1960, 1966). Exhaustive and enlightening studies dealing with the medieval and modern periods, respectively.

ARABIA AND MUHAMMAD

DE PLANHOL, XAVIER. *The World of Islam* (Cornell University Press, 1958). Essay on the impact of geography upon Islam.

FISHER, W. B. *The Middle East,* 5th ed. (Methuen, 1963). The standard detailed work on the geography of the area.

CHEJNE, ANWAR. *The Arabic Language* (University of Minnesota, 1969). Helpful evaluation of its role in history.

GABRIELI, F. *Muhammad and the Conquests of Islam* (McGraw-Hill, 1968). Recent brief account with a valuable bibliographical discussion.

CARLYLE, T. "The Hero as Prophet," in *On Heroes, Hero-Worship and the Heroic in History* (London: Oxford University Press, 1946). This celebrated lecture, delivered in 1840, was a pioneering effort at a sympathetic appraisal of Muhammad.

ANDRAE, TOR. *Mohammed: The Man and His Faith,* rev. ed. (Barnes & Noble, 1955). Sympathetic brief account by a Lutheran bishop.

WATT, W. M. *Muhammad Prophet and Statesman* (Oxford University Press, 1961). Persuasively argued sociological interpretation; based on the author's more detailed monographs, *Muhammad at Mecca* and *Muhammad at Medina.*

RODINSON, M. *Mohammed* (Pantheon, 1971). Lively and enlightening biography by an agnostic scholar.

GUILLAUME, A. (ed.). *The Life of Muhammad* (Oxford University Press, 1955). Translation of the classical Muslim life of the Prophet.

GLUBB, J. B. *The Life and Times of Muhammad* (Stein and Day, 1970). Sympathetic biography by a professed Christian; old-fashioned in tone but with valuable insights from the author, the former commander of the Arab Legion.

TORREY, C. C. *The Jewish Foundation of Islam* (Ktav, 1967). New edition of a controversial work stressing Muhammad's debt to Judaism.

BELL, RICHARD. *The Origin of Islam in Its Christian Environment* (Frank Cass, 1968). Reprint of lectures first published in 1926; scholarly assessment of the Christian contribution to the teachings of the Prophet and the Islamic tradition.

THE TEACHINGS OF ISLAM AND THE PILLARS OF THE FAITH

WATT, W. M. *Bell's Introduction to the Qur'an* (Edinburgh University Press, 1970). Complete revision and enlargement of a scholarly study published a generation ago by Richard Bell.

ARBERRY, A. J. *The Koran Interpreted* (Macmillan, 1955). Perhaps the most successful attempt to preserve some of the literary quality of the original in translation.

PICKTHALL, M. M. *The Meaning of the Glorious Koran* (Mentor, 1953). A translation by an English convert to Islam.

DAWOOD, N. J. *The Koran: A New Translation* (Penguin, 1956). Readable version with the suras rearranged in approximate chronological sequence.

BELL, RICHARD. *The Qur'an, Translated with a Critical Rearrangement of the Surahs,* 2 vols. (University of Edinburgh Press, 1960). Scholarly dissection and reconstruction.

GUILLAUME, A. *The Traditions of Islam* (Khayats, 1966). Scholarly evaluation of the hadiths and their role.

CRAGG, KENNETH. *The Call of the Minaret* (Oxford University Press, 1956). Sympathetic, though slightly condescending, introduction by a well-informed Christian scholar.

VON GRUNEBAUM, G. E. *Muhammadan Festivals* (Abelard-Schuman, 1958). Enlightening vignettes of major religious holidays.

JAMALI, MOHAMMED FADHEL. *Letters on Islam* (Oxford University Press, 1965). An Iraqi statesman, imprisoned after the revolution of 1958, reflects on the significance of the Pillars of the Faith.

KAMAL, AHMAD. *The Sacred Journey* (Allen & Unwin, 1964). A modern Muslim's impressive account of the hajj and its significance.

ASAD, MUHAMMAD. *The Road to Mecca* (Simon & Schuster, 1954). Autobiography of a German Jew who was converted to Islam and rose to high office in Pakistan.

THE LAW AND THE STATE

SCHACHT, JOSEPH. *Origins of Muhammadan Jurisprudence* (Clarendon, 1950). The standard authority on the subject. Its interpretations may be revised in the light of the more recent work of N. J. Coulson.

COULSON, N. J. *A History of Islamic Law* (Edinburgh University Press, 1964). A lucid survey from the beginnings to the present.

MACDONALD, D. B. *Development of Muslim Theology, Jurisprudence, and Constitutional Theory* (1903). Instructive and stimulating, though somewhat outdated in interpretations.

WELLHAUSEN, J. *The Arab Kingdom and Its Fall* (Khayats, 1963). A full narrative of the rise and fall of the Umayyad caliphate.

GLUBB, J. B. *The Great Arab Conquests* (Prentice-Hall, 1963); *The Empire of the Arabs* (Hodder and Stoughton, 1963); *The Course of Empire* (Hodder and Stoughton, 1965). Leisurely accounts of Arab expansion by a soldier thoroughly acquainted with the Arabs.

LEVY, REUBEN. *The Social Structure of Islam* (Cambridge University Press, 1965). Detailed analysis of the effects of Islamic beliefs and institutions on social developments.

SHABAN, M. A. *The Abbasid Revolution* (Cambridge University, Press, 1971). Revisionist interpretation asserting that the main support of the revolution came from Arabs. Shaban has also published *Islamic History A.D. 600–750. A New Interpretation* (Cambridge University Press, 1971).

BOSWORTH, C. E. *The Islamic Dynasties* (Edinburgh University Press, 1967). A useful genealogical handbook.

WATT, W. M. *A History of Islamic Spain* (Edinburgh University Press, 1965). A good brief introduction.

BOYLE, J. A. (ed.). *The Cambridge History of Iran*, vol. V. *The Saljuq and Mongol Periods* (Cambridge University Press, 1968). With contributions by nearly a dozen experts.

ORTHODOXY AND HETERODOXY

DONALDSON, D. M. *The Shi'ite Religion* (Luzac, 1933). A detailed though rather uncritical study.

LEWIS, BERNARD. *The Assassins* (Weidenfeld and Nicolson, 1967). Admirable assessment of this exotic offshoot, with considerable information also on the parent Ismailis.

HODGSON, M. G. *The Order of the Assassins* (Mouton, 1955). Detailed study based on a doctoral dissertation.

SALEM, ELIE ADIB. "Political Theory and Institutions of the Khawarij." *The Johns Hopkins University Studies in Historical and Political Science*, LXXIV (1956). Instructive monograph on the Kharijites.

AFNAN, RUHI M. *The Revelation of Baha'u'llah and the Bab* (Philosophical Library, 1970). A comprehensive introduction to Babism and the Bahai faith.

BROWNE, E. G. *Materials for the Study of the Babi Religion* (Cambridge University Press, 1961). By the only European scholar to have personal acquaintance with Bahaullah; centered more on the growings pains of the Bahai faith than on Babism.

ESSLEMONT, J. E. *Baha'u'llah and the New Era,* 3rd ed. (Pyramid Books, 1970). A lucid introduction to the Bahai faith by an ardent believer.

HITTI, P. K. *The Origins of the Druze People and Religion* (Columbia University Press, 1928). Informative monograph on a controversial subject.

SUFISM

NICHOLSON, R. A. *The Mystics of Islam* (Routledge & Kegan Paul, 1963). Reissue of a study of the Sufi pathway first published in 1914, with abundant quotations from the Sufis themselves.

ARBERRY, A. J. *Sufism: An Account of the Mystics of Islam* (Allen & Unwin, 1950). Comprehensive introductory survey by the scholar who succeeded Nicholson as Professor of Arabic at Cambridge University. He has translated a medieval Persian memorial to Sufi saints: *Muslim Saints and Mystics* (University of Chicago Press, 1966), an excellent introduction to the popular literature of Sufism.

MACDONALD, D. B. *The Religious Attitude and Life in Islam* (Khayats, 1965). Lectures delivered in 1906, a pioneering attempt to distinguish between systematic theology and popular religion.

SMITH, MARGARET. (ed.). *Readings from the Mystics of Islam* (Luzac, 1950). Brief selections from some of the Sufi writers.

TRIMINGHAM, J. S. *The Sufi Orders in Islam* (Clarendon Press, 1971). Comprehensive scholarly study.

SHAH, IDRIES. *The Sufis* (Doubleday, 1964). Popular exposition by a Sufi, emphasizing the common denominators among mystics of all faiths.

RICE, CYPRIAN. *The Persian Sufis* (Allen & Unwin, 1964). Interpretation employing the language of Christian mysticism.

BIRGE, J. K. *The Bektashi Order of Dervishes* (Luzac, 1937). A detailed study of the Turkish brotherhood by an American Protestant missionary very familiar with the Turkish scene.

LANE, E. W. *Manners and Customs of the Modern Egyptians* (Everyman, 1923). Includes celebrated eye-witness reports of dervish activities more than a century ago.

WATT, W. M. *Muslim Intellectual* (Edinburgh University Press, 1963). A fascinating study of al-Ghazali.

PHILOSOPHY AND SCIENCE

WALZER, RICHARD. *Greek into Arabic* (Harvard University Press, 1962). Scholarly essays on the relationship between Greek and Islamic philosophy. The first essay in the volume is an excellent introduction to the subject. More detailed information on the translators is provided in R. M. Haddad, *Syrian Christians in Muslim Society* (Princeton University Press, 1970).

WATT, W. MONTGOMERY. *Islamic Philosophy and Theology* (Edinburgh University Press, 1962), and *Islamic Political Thought* (Edinburgh University Press, 1968). Illuminating introductions to important topics.

ROSENTHAL, E. I. J. *Political Thought in Medieval Islam* (Cambridge University Press, 1958). A thoughtful study in detail.

ROSENTHAL, E. I. J. *Knowledge Triumphant* (Brill, 1970). Scholarly work stressing the ascendancy of the concept of knowledge both among the medieval ulema and in spiritual and social life.

FAKHRY, MAJID. *A History of Islamic Philosophy* (Columbia University Press, 1970). Useful introductory survey.

PETERS, F. E. *Aristotle and the Arabs* (New York University Press, 1969). Study of the unsettling effects of Aristotelianism on Islamic intellectual life.

ARBERRY, A. H. (trans.). *The Spiritual Physick of Rhazes* (John Murray, 1950). Ar-Razi's pioneering recommendations for emotional therapy delightfully presented.

MAHDI, MAHSIN. (trans.). *Al-Farabi's Philosophy of Plato and Aristotle* (Free Press, 1962). With an important introduction to a controversial figure in Muslim intellectual history.

AFNAN, SOHEIL M. *Avicenna: His Life and Works* (Allen & Unwin, 1958). Clear and comprehensive study of a key intellectual figure. May be supplemented by the lectures commemorating Avicenna's thousandth birthday in G. M. Wickens (ed.). *Avicenna: Scientist and Philosopher* (Luzac, 1952).

HOURANI, G. F. (trans.). *Averroes: On the Harmony of Religion and Philosophy* (Luzac, 1961). With a very informative introduction.

IBN-KHALDUN. *The Muqaddimah* (Princeton University Press, 1969). Translated by F. Rosenthal, edited and abridged by N. H. Dawood. Well-chosen excerpts from ibn-Khaldun's philosophy of history.

MAHDI, MUHSIN. *Ibn Khaldun's Philosophy of History* (University of Chicago Press, 1964). Perceptive analysis.

MYERS, E. A. *Arabic Thought and the Western World* (Frederick Ungar, 1964). A concise survey of Islamic scholars who influenced Western science and culture.

NASR, SEYYED HOSSEIN. *Science and Civilization in Islam* (Harvard University Press, 1968). Stimulating and suggestive study, which has provoked controversy because of its sympathetic attitude toward the occult aspects of Islamic science.

BROWNE, E. G. *Arabian Medicine* (Cambridge University Press, 1921). Four delightful lectures by a famous writer on Persian literature and history.

ELGOOD, C. *A Medical History of Persia and the Eastern Caliphate* (Cambridge University Press, 1951). A detailed survey by a physician, from the beginnings to the present century.

THE ARTS

GRUBE, E. J. *The World of Islam* (McGraw-Hill, n.d.). Comprehensive and suggestive survey by a ranking expert; superbly illustrated.

RICE, DAVID TALBOT. *Islamic Art* (Praeger, 1965). A sound introduction, profusely illustrated.

RICE, DAVID TALBOT. *Islamic Painting* (Edinburgh University Press, 1971). A specialized study.

RICE, TAMARA TALBOT. *The Seljuks in Asia Minor* (Thames and Hudson, 1961). With a good chapter on the Seljuks' artistic achievements.

HILL, DEREK, and GRABAR, OTTO. *Islamic Architecture and Its Decoration* (University of Chicago Press, 1964). Handsomely illustrated essay stressing the Seljuk contribution.

HOAG, J. D. *Western Islamic Architecture* (Prentice-Hall, 1963). Brief survey of Spain, North Africa, Egypt, and Turkey.

WILSON, R. P. *Islamic Art* (Macmillan, 1957). Less comprehensive than the title suggests, but with excellent illustrations of ceramics and weaving.

DAVIS, FANNY. *The Palace of Topkapi in Istanbul* (Scribner, 1970). Detailed and generously illustrated discussion of this important Ottoman complex.

ETTINGHAUSEN, R. *Arab Painting* (Skira, 1962). Instructive review, with beautiful illustrations.

MC MULLAN, J. V. *Islamic Carpets* (Near Eastern Art Research Center, 1965). A great collector discusses his hobby. Spectacular illustrations.

KURAN, APTULLAH. *The Mosque in Early Ottoman Architecture* (University of Chicago Press, 1968). A thorough and informative scholarly review.

LITERATURE

GIBB, H. A. R. *Arabic Literature*, 2nd ed. (Clarendon, 1963). Admirable introduction.

NICHOLSON, R. A. *A Literary History of the Arabs* (Cambridge University Press, 1962). An older and longer account.

BROWNE, E. G. *A Literary History of the Persians*, 4 vols. (Cambridge University Press, 1928). Exhaustive account by a great expert.

LEVY, REUBEN. *An Introduction to Persian Literature* (Columbia University Press, 1969). Brief and excellent.

ARBERRY, A. J. (ed.). *Persian Poems* (Everyman, 1954). Anthology of English translations.

GRAVES, ROBERT. and ALI-SHAH, OMAR. *The Original Rubaiyyat of Omar Khayaam* (Doubleday, 1968). Strongly revisionist version defending Omar as a Sufi.

THE MODERN CHALLENGE

GIBB, H. A. R. and BOWEN, HAROLD. *Islamic Society and the West*, vol. I (Oxford University Press, 1957). Detailed scholarly survey of the Ottoman institutions confronting the modern challenge.

LEWIS, BERNARD. *The Emergence of Modern Turkey,* 2nd ed. (Oxford University Press). Thorough and well-balanced assessment of developments in the nineteenth century and the first half of the twentieth.

BERKES, NIYAZI. *The Development of Secularism in Turkey* (McGill University Press, 1964). Thorough and informative review by a Turk.

ROSENTHAL, E. I. J. *Islam in the Modern National State* (Cambridge University Press, 1965). Solid scholarly study touching on many states.

SMITH, W. C. *Islam in Modern History* (Princeton University Press, 1957). Quirky and provocative survey.

KEDDIE, NIKKI R. *An Islamic Response to Imperialism* (University of California Press, 1968). Scholarly translation and assessment of Afghani's political and religious writings.

ALGAR, HAMAD. *Religion and State in Iran, 1785–1906* (University of California Press, 1970). Valuable analysis of the political role of the Persian ulema.

ADAMS, C. C. *Islam and Modernism in Egypt* (Oxford University Press, 1933). Focused on Muhammad Abduh. Its conclusions should be compared with more recent studies such as H. A. R. Gibb, *Modern Trends in Islam* (University of Chicago Press, 1947), Albert Hourani, *Arabic Thought in the Liberal Ages* (Oxford University Press, 1962), and Sylvia Haim, *Arab Nationalism* (University of California Press, 1962).

HALPERN, M. *The Politics of Social Change in the Middle East and North Africa* (Princeton University Press, 1963). Very suggestive and informed survey.

HUSAINI, ISHAK MUSA. *The Moslem Brethren* (Khayats, 1956). Subjective analysis by a Muslim; more enlightening than more recent scholarly studies, of which the best is James Mitchell, *The Society of the Muslim Brothers* (Oxford University Press, 1969).

BERGER, MORROE. *Islam in Egypt Today* (Cambridge University Press, 1970). Stresses popular religious movements.

GEERTZ, CLIFFORD. *Islam Observed* (Yale University Press, 1968). Most informative analysis of religious developments at the opposite poles of the Islamic world, Morocco and Indonesia.

KRITZECK, H., and LEWIS, W. H. (eds.). *Islam in Africa* (Van Nostrand Reinhold, 1969). Useful survey, with chapters by many different experts.

ABBOTT, FREELAND. *Islam and Pakistan* (Cornell University Press, 1968). Thoughtful review of the vicissitudes of Islam on the subcontinent.

AHMAD, AZIZ. *Islamic Modernism in India and Pakistan* (Oxford University Press, 1967). A more detailed analysis.

Abbas, Shah, 137, 144
Abbasid caliphate, 55, 65–69, 73, 78–79, 98, 119–120, 140–141
Abd-al-Malik, 133
Abd-ar-Rahman III, 66
Abduh, Muhammad, 163
Abdul Aziz, 159
Abdul Hamid II, 68–69, 162
Abraham, 6, 16–17, 30, 47–49
Abu-Bakr, 59–60, 62
Abu-Talib, 17, 21, 60
Adam, 6, 47, 127
Adultery, 58
Afghanistan, 55
Africa, 6, 12, 55, 155
(*See also* North Africa; West Africa)
Agha Khan, 80
Agra, India, 135, 137
Ahmadiya, the, 95–96
Aisha, 59
Al-Adawiya, Rabia, quoted, 87
Al-Afghani, Jamal ad-Din, 162–163
Al-Ashari, Abul Hasan, 108
Al-Assad, Hafiz, General, 81
Alawis, the, 80–81
Al-Azhar university, 120, 162–163
Al-Badawi, Ahmad, 96
Al-Banna, Hasan, 160–161
Albigensians, 74
Al-Bukhari, 31–32
Alchemists, 127–129
Alchemy, 126–129
Aleppo, 67, 137
Alexander the Great, 86
Al-Farabi, 110–111, 119, 130
Algebra, 123–125
Algeria, 72, 157
Al-Ghazali, 98–101, 108, 114–115, 130, 147, 152
quoted, 91–92, 99–100

Al-Gilani, Abd-al-Qadir, 93
Alhambra, the, 136, 142
Ali, caliph, 60, 64, 71–76, 81, 84, 105–106
Ali, Muhammad, 159
Ali-Shah, Omar, 152
Al-Jebel, sheik, 80
Al-Khuwarizmi, 123–124
Allah, 2, 15, 18, 20, 24–26, 36–39, 52, 71, 87–89, 91, 93, 106–107, 160
Alms, giving of, 43–44
Al-Wahab, Muhammad ibn Abd, 158
Anatolia, 10, 62, 67–69, 94, 97, 143, 164
Anesthesia, 123
Aqsa Mosque, 133–134
Arabesque, 3, 139
Arabia, 5–15, 23–24, 26, 61, 64, 72, 77, 155, 158–159
Arabian Nights, The, 3, 66, 147
Arabic, 2–3, 8–10, 26, 64, 104, 119–120, 164–165
Arabic manuscripts, 103
Arabs, 3, 7–8, 13–15, 23, 30, 50, 54, 61–63, 78, 124, 139, 157, 162
Arafat, 47–48, 50
Aramaeans, 8
Aramco, 159
Architects, Muslim, 3, 146
Architecture, 132–144
Byzantine, 133–134
Islamic, 135–145
Turkish, 142–143
Aristotle, 106, 110–111, 115
Armenians, 94, 158
Ar-Razi, 109–110, 119, 121, 126, 129–130
quoted, 109, 121
writings of, 109, 122

Arts, the, 132–146
Asceticism, 87
Asharites, the, 108–109, 115, 158
Assassins, the, 79–80
Astrology, 126–129
Astronomers, 124–126
Astronomy, 125
Atatürk, Kemal, 164–165
Averroes, 114–116, 119
Avicenna, 112–115, 119–120, 122, 128, 130, 147
  quoted, 112–114, 129

Bab, the, 83–85
Babis, the, 83–84
Badr, 24–25, 44
Baghdad, 55, 65–68, 93, 98–100, 120, 123
Bahai, the, 83–85
Bahaullah, 83–84
Bairam, festival of, 45
Balance of power, shifting, 10–12
Balkans, the, 62
Banu Hashim clan, 16–18, 21
Barbary coast, 60–61
Bedouins, 5, 8, 10, 12–13, 23–25, 62, 159
Begging, 44
Bektashis, the, 96
Berbers, 60–61, 66, 68, 72, 78, 96–97
Bismillah, the, 37, 138
Boccaccio, 3
Body, the, four humors of, 128
Brick, 143
Brotherhoods, 92–93
  liabilities and assets of, 96–98
  Muslim (*see* Muslim Brotherhood)
  rustic, 93–96
  urban, 93–94
Byzantine Empire, 25, 62, 94, 104
Byzantium, 10–13, 61, 68

Cairo, 67–68, 78–79, 81, 95, 98, 120, 134, 137, 141, 161
Caliphates, the, 58–60, 64, 70, 72, 79, 105
  end of, 68–69, 160
Caliphs, 59–60, 63–67, 72, 78–79, 105–106, 162
Calligraphy, 139
Canon of Medicine, The, Avicenna, 122
Caravans, 6, 13, 16, 24
  pilgrim, 49
Caravanseries (hans), 137, 143

Carlyle, Thomas, quoted, 28–30, 35
Carmathians, 78
Catholicism, 86, 114, 116
Chaucer, 3
Chemistry, 129
China, 60
  communist, 155–156
Christianity, 1–2, 5, 11, 14–15, 17, 74, 81, 84, 89, 92–93, 96, 106, 111, 126, 157
Christians, 3, 12, 30, 58, 68, 82, 87, 94, 104, 115, 119–120, 141
Church, the, 59, 159
Citadels, 137
Clans, 13–14, 18, 21–22
Clocks, 125–126
Colonialism, 154–155
Communism, 156–157
Communists, 156
Comte, Auguste, 163
Conversion and converts, 58, 63–64, 66, 72
Copts, 158
Cordova, 66–67, 134, 141
Crusades, the, 67–68, 79
Ctesiphon, 140

Damascus, 6, 49, 60, 64–65, 67, 69, 100, 116, 133–136
Darazi, 81
Death, fear of, 110
Dervishes, 91–96, 131, 151, 165
  howling, 95
  whirling, 94
Determinism, 105
Dhikrs, 91–95, 130
Dietary restrictions, 56
Dissidents, 70–72
Divorce, 57
Dome of the Rock, 64, 132–135
Druzes, the, 81–83
Dualism, 73–74

Eden, 47, 127
Egypt, 8, 10–12, 45, 49, 55, 60–62, 64, 66–68, 78–80, 96, 116, 155, 160, 165
Elements, the, 127–128
Emerson, quoted, 152
Emirs, 66
Epicureanism, 104
Epileptics, 19
Esther, Queen, 147
Ethiopia, 12–13
Ettinghausen, Richard, quoted, 133
Euphrates, the, 11–12

Europe, 68
  (*See also* names of countries)
Eve, 47

Fadayan Islam, 160
Faith, 71, 81, 100–101, 105, 109
  confession of, 39–40
  pillars of, 39–52
  syncretistic, 74, 78, 80, 88, 103
Faqirs, 91, 97
Farouk, King, 161
Fasting, 44–45
Fatihah, the, 41
Fatima, 60
Fatimids, the, 66, 68, 78–79, 81, 98, 120
Feast of Sacrifice, 48
Ferdinand and Isabella, 68
Fertile Crescent, the, 5–8, 10–12, 14, 25, 63, 67, 73, 80, 86
Fetwas, 54
Firdausi, 152
Fitzgerald, Edward, quoted, 152
Flowers, 145
France, 3, 61
Free will, 105
Friday, 42
Friday Mosque, 143–144

Gabriel, 6, 17–19, 37, 48
Galen, 121
Gardening, 145
Gaza, 6
Genesis, 8, 16, 48
Geography, 125
Geometry, 123, 125
Ghana, 97
Ghassanids, the, 11, 13–14
Ghazals, 150–151
Ghaznawids, the, 98
Gibb, Sir Hamilton, 98, 101
  quoted, 88, 99
Gibraltar, 61
Giralda Tower, 141–142
Gnosticism, 73, 78, 83, 87, 103, 106, 126
God, 30–31, 35, 42–43, 71, 74, 82, 87–89, 91, 93, 97, 106–108, 110, 114, 126–127, 138, 151
  man and, 29, 36–38, 75, 105, 158–159
  surrender to, 39
  unity of, 106
Goddesses, 14
Granada, 136, 142
Grand Book of Music, al-Farabi, 130

Grand mufti, 69
Graves, Robert, 153
Great Mosque, the, 46–47, 64, 133–134
Greece, 103–105, 124
Greeks, 102, 158
Grube, E. J., 137, 142
  quoted, 135–136

Hadiths, 31–32, 36, 40, 52–53, 138–139, 147
  validity of, 54
Hafiz, 152
Hagar, 47
Haifa, 83–84
Hajj, the, 46–51, 82, 100 163
  number of pilgrims making, 49–50
Hajjid, 50
Hakim, caliph, 81–82
Hanafi, law, 55
Hanbali, law, 56–57, 108, 160
Hanifs (ascetics), 15, 17, 30
Haram ash-Sherif, the, 134
Harun ar-Rashid, 66, 103, 140
Hasan, 73–77
Hashimites, the, 16, 21
Hashish, 79
Hasidim, the, 86
Heaven, 2, 107
  (*See also* Paradise)
Hebrews, 8
Hegira, the, 23
Hejaz, the, 6–7, 13–14, 22, 49, 60
Hejaz Railway, 49, 69, 163
Hell, Muslim, 34–35, 105, 107–108
Heresy, 71, 74, 116
Heretics, 11–12, 85
Herod, 134
Heterodoxy, 70–85
Hindus, 97, 156
Hitti, Philip K., quoted, 146–147
House of Wisdom, 103, 120, 123
Human conduct and human rights, 56–58
Hungary, 68
Hussein, 73–77

Ibn-Hanbal, Ahmad, 106
Ibn-Khaldun, 116–118
  quoted, 128
Ibn-Saud, 50, 57, 159
Imams, 42, 59, 74–76, 83, 96
  hidden, 76–78, 80–83
Imperialism, 162
Incense, 6
Incoherence of the Incoherence, The, Averroes, 115
Incoherence of Philosophy, The, al-Ghazali, 99, 114–115

India, 3, 6, 55, 60, 77, 80, 97–98, 135, 155–156
Indians, 157
Indonesia, 55, 98, 154–156
Inheritance, 57
Iqbal, Muhammad, quoted, 97
Iran, 10, 64, 67, 76, 84, 137, 143, 155, 160
    (*See also* Persia)
Iraq, 16, 55, 60, 62, 64–67, 73, 76–79, 124, 140
Isaac, 48
Isfahan, 137, 143–144
Ishmael, 16, 47–48
Islam, 20–21, 23, 26, 29–30, 32–33, 36, 39, 42, 59, 64, 70, 86, 96–98
    culture of, 132
    expansion of, 60–63
    medieval, 98, 154
    modern, 154, 162–165
    inner crisis of, 158–159
    sacred law of, 52
    Shia, 72–76, 83, 96, 106
    Spanish, 115
    teachings of, 27–38
    Western image of, 1–4, 10, 70, 102
Islamic calendar, 23*n*., 44, 46
Islamic tradition, 154
Ismail, 77–78
Ismailia, 160–161
Ismailis, the, 77–80, 120, 126
Israel, 56, 83–84
Israelis, the, 50
Istanbul, 68, 136, 146, 163
Ivory, 6
Iznik, 145–146

Jamaat-i-Islam, 160
Jebel Alawi, the, 81
Jebel Druze, the, 81
Jerusalem, 24–25, 64, 67, 133, 135
Jesus, 1, 5, 11, 27, 36, 75–76
    (*See also* Messiah)
Jewels, 6
Jews, 3, 5, 7, 12, 23–25, 30, 56, 58, 119, 158
Jidda, 49
Jihad, the, 24–25, 61, 72, 163
Jinn, 14
Jordan, 16, 56, 63
Judaism, 1, 5, 7, 14–15, 17, 86
Judeo-Christian tradition, 1, 5
Judgment Day, 88, 105, 110
    (*See also* Last Judgment)
Jundishapur, 120–121

Kaaba, the, 6, 14, 16, 22, 25–26, 46–47, 78, 133

Kalila and Dimna, 147-149
Kamal, Ahmad, quoted, 47–48
Karbala, 73, 75
Khadija, 17, 20
Khalifa, 92
Kharijites, the, 71–72, 105, 159
Kizilbashi, 81
Konya, 94, 131, 143
Koran, the, 3, 9–10, 19–20, 27–41, 43–44, 54, 107, 110, 160
    English version of, 30
    as literature, 30, 146–147
    and the Sharia, 52–53
    structure of, 29
Kufa, 60
Kurds, the, 67

Lakhmids, the, 11–14
Languages, Arabic (*see* Arabic)
    Aramaic, 8, 11, 64
    Hebrew, 8–9
    Semitic, 8
    Syriac, 104
Last Judgment, the, 30, 34–38
    (*See also* Judgment Day)
Law, and the state, 52–69
League of the Virtuous, the, 18
Lebanon, 56, 77, 81–83
Lewis, Bernard, 61
    quoted, 50, 62–63, 71
Liberalism, 106
Literature, 9, 16
    folk, 149
    Koran as, 30, 146–147
    poetic (*see* Poetry)
    prose, 146–149
    Sufi, 89–91
Liwans, 140, 143–144, 146
Love, 151
Lucretius, 104

Macdonald, Duncan B., 106
    quoted, 102
Mahdi, the, 76, 78
Maimonides, 119
Majlis, the, 13
Malay peninsula, 98
Maliki, law, 55
Malikshah, Sultan, 143
Mameluks, 66, 68, 80
Mamun, caliph, 103, 106, 140
Man, and God, 29, 36–38, 75, 105
    qualities of, 117
    suspended, 113–114
    universal, 112
Manicheans and Manicheism, 74
Marabouts, 96–97, 158
Marib dike, 12

Marriage, 58, 164
plural, 53, 57, 82
Martyrs, 73
Marx, 156
Mathematics, 123–126
Mauretania, 61
Mecca, 6–7, 15, 17–18, 24–26, 29, 34, 41, 56, 75, 78, 138, 159
ascendency of, 13–14
Muhammad in, 20–23
pilgrimages to, 46–51
Medicine, 120–123
Medina, 6–7, 30, 42, 49, 53, 55–56, 60, 69, 75
Muhammad in, 23–26, 43–44, 48, 71
Medina, the, 110
Mediterranean, the, 5, 13, 49, 67
Mesopotamia, 11, 65, 140
Messiah, the, 39–40
Metals, 127, 129
Mevlana, 94
Mevleviya, the, 94, 151
Middle East, the, 10–11, 50, 55, 68, 87, 123, 155, 165
Mihrab, the, 41, 138
Mina, 48–49
Minarets, 40, 137, 141, 143
Missionaries, Ismaili, 78, 80–81
Sufi, 98
Moharram, month of, 73, 75
Mongols, the, 68, 80
Monophysites, 11–12, 14, 104
Moors, 61, 68
Morocco, 61, 66, 77, 96, 120, 158
Mosaics, 133–134
Mosques, 3, 27, 41–42, 46, 132–134, 137–138, 140–141, 145–146
decoration of, 138–139
Persian, 140, 143
Mount of Mercy, 47
Muawiya, 60, 64, 71, 73
Muezzin, the, 40, 137
Muftis, 54–55
Muhammad, 1, 5–7, 12, 15–28, 31–34, 36, 39–40, 42–44, 46, 52–62, 70–71, 74–75, 85, 88, 93, 133, 138–139, 150, 156
ancestry of, 16–17
becomes a prophet, 18–20
death of, 25
in Medina, 22–26
messages of, 18–20
preaching and persecution of, 20–22
Muhammad at Mecca, Watts, 18
Muqaddimah, ibn-Khaldun, 117–118

Murjiites, 105–106
Music, 129–131
Music and Ecstasy, al-Ghazali, 130
Musical instruments, 130–131
Muslim Brotherhood, the, 160–162
Muslims, 1–3, 8–10, 12, 20–22, 24–25, 29–32, 36–38, 47–48, 50, 63–65, 67, 69–72, 102
and confession of faith, 39–40
law of, 52–60
medieval, 3
non-Arab, 65–66
and non-Muslims, 119
number of, in 1971, 155
and prayer, 40–44
present-day, 154–155, 162–163
Mutazilites, the, 105–108
Muwashshah, the, 150
example of, 150–151
Mysticism, 103, 114

Naqshbandiya, the, 93–94
Nasser, Gamal Abdel, 161–162
quoted, 50–51
Nationalism, 156–157
Arab, 7–8, 22
Nature, qualities of, 128
Navigation, 125
Navigators, Muslim, 2
Necessary being, the, 113
Neoplatonists, 103, 111, 115
Nestorians, 11–12, 14, 104, 110–111, 120
New Testament, 27, 30, 32
Nile, the, 96
Nizam al-Mulk, 79
Nominalists, 115
North Africa, 55, 61, 66, 68, 78, 97, 141, 155
Numbers, science of, 124

Oases, 7
Old Testament, 24–25, 27, 30, 32
Oman, 72
Omar Khayyam, 123–124, 152
quoted, 153
Optics, 123, 125
Oriental rugs, 142, 144–145
Orphans, 53
Orthodoxy, 70–85, 93, 98
Osmanli, the, 68
Ottoman Empire, 55–56, 68–69, 94, 96, 158–159, 163–164
Ottomans, 142–143, 145–146

Pakistan, 55, 77, 98, 160
Palaces, 132, 136, 139–140, 142, 144
Palestine, 7, 10, 48, 79, 140

Palestinian War of 1948, 161
Pan-Islam, 162–163
Paradise, 2, 34–35, 105
    (*See also* Heaven)
Pathways to truth, 55–56, 70
Persia, 11–13, 60, 62, 66–67, 73–
    74, 79–80, 83, 96, 98, 100,
    113, 120, 133, 142–145, 162
    (*See also* Iran)
Persians, 66, 112, 120–121, 123–
    124, 126, 152
Philosophers, Muslim, 3, 108–118
    Greek influence on, 102–111, 116
Philosopher's stone, 129
Philosophy, 102–118
    Greek influence on, 102–111, 116
    and religion, 115
    Western, 116
Physicians, 120–121, 128
Physics, 125
Pilgrim's way, the, 89–91
Pillars of the Faith, 39–52, 72, 80
Plato, 109, 111
Poetry, 3, 9–10, 114, 130–132, 149–
    153
Poets, 14, 104, 124, 150–152
Poitiers, Battle of, 61
Politics, 58, 110–111
Polygamy (*see* Marriage, plural)
Pottery, 141
Poverty, 89, 91
Prayer rugs, 42
Prayers, 2, 40–44
    communal, 42
Priests, 14
Promise and threat, doctrine of,
    107
Prophet, the (*see* Muhammad)
Prostration, prayer and, 41
Protestantism, 86, 159
Ptolemy, 125
Purification, 40–41, 46
Puritans, 70, 72, 105
Pythagoras, 130

Qadiriya, the, 93
Qadis (judges), 54
Qanun, 58
Qasida, the, 149
Quraish, the, 12–13, 16, 21–22, 24,
    72

Ramadan, 24, 34, 44–46, 48, 80,
    82, 165
Rashidun caliphs, 59–60, 70
Rationalism, 114, 126, 163
Realists, 115

Reason, 115
    faith and, 101, 109
Red Sea, the, 6, 13
Religion, 70
    philosophy and, 115
    pre-Islamic, 14–15
Repentance, 89
Revival of Religious Sciences, The,
    al-Ghazali, 100
Rifaiya, the, 94–96
Roman emperors, 10
Romans, 104
Rubaiyat, the, 152–153
Rumi, Jalal ud-din, 152
    quoted, 151

Sa'di, 152
Sadiya, the, 95
Safavids, the, 137, 143–146
Salaam, 35
Saladin, 67–68, 79, 119, 137
Samarkand, 120
Samarra, 76, 83, 140–141
Santa Sophia, 146
Sarah, 16–17
Sasanids, 10–12, 60, 62
Satan, 48
Saudi Arabia, 49–50, 56–57, 69,
    72, 159
Saudis, the, 159
Scholastics, 114–115
Schools, 143–144
Science, 119–131
    pseudo-, 126
Scientists, 2, 119, 130
Secularism, 163–165
Seljuks, 67, 79, 94, 108, 137, 142–
    144
Semites, 7–8
Seville, 141
Shafii, law, 55
Shahada, the, 39, 41
Shapur, emperor, 120
Sharia, the, 52–58, 69, 80, 100, 106,
    158, 163–165
Sheiks, 13, 42, 59, 63, 80, 92, 96–
    97
Shem, 7
Shiism, 72–76, 88, 93, 98, 103, 111
    Twelver, 76–77, 83
Shiites, the, 64, 66, 73, 75–78, 81,
    83, 126
Shiraz, 83
Sicily, 61, 78
Sinan, 146
Sira, the 16–17, 21, 31
Slavery, 58
Socrates, 109

Souls, 110
    transmigration of, 81–82
    transmutation of, 127
Southeast Asia, 154–155
Soviet Union, 155–157
Spain, 2–3, 61, 66, 68, 119–120, 124, 136, 140–141, 150
Spencer, Herbert, 163
Spices, 6
Spiritual Physick, The, al-Razi, 109, 122
State, the, 110
    church and, 59
    ideal, 110–111
    and the law, 52–69
Stoicism, 104
Suez Canal, 49, 160
Sufis, the, 85, 87–89, 126, 158
    literature of, 89–91, 151–152
Sufism, 85–101, 103, 115, 153, 158, 160, 165
Sukarno, President, 156
Suleiman the Magnificent, 133, 146
Sunna, the, 54, 70
Sunnis, the, 70–71, 73, 75, 77, 79–80, 82, 88, 93, 96, 98, 108
Suras, 29–30, 37, 39, 41, 53
Surgery, 123
Suspended man, the, 113–114
Syncretism, 74, 78, 80, 88, 103
Syria, 10–12, 17, 49, 56, 60, 62–64, 66–68, 71, 78–83, 87, 140
Syriac language, 104

Taj Mahal, the, 135–136
Tamerlane, 116, 120
Tanta, 96
Tanzania, 72
Tariq, 61
Tariqa, the, 88–92
Textiles, 6
Theft, 58, 159
Thomas Aquinas, Saint, 114
Tiles, 143, 145–146
Toledo, 120
Tolerance, 58, 84, 102, 106
Topkapi palace, 136, 145
Tower of Babel, 141
Tribes, 13, 22, 72

Trigonometry, 124
Troubadours, 150
Tunisia, 45, 66, 72, 78, 116, 134
Turkestan, 66
Turkey, 67, 69, 94, 143, 155, 163–165
Turks, the, 66–68, 96–98, 137, 154, 158
    (*See also* Ottomans; Seljuks)
Twelvers, the, 76–77, 83

Ulema, the, 53–55, 57, 93, 98, 100, 105–108, 115, 128, 158, 165
Umayyads, the, 60, 63–66, 68, 72–73, 119, 135–136, 140–141
Umma, the, 22–23, 26, 58–59, 110
United States, Bahai in 84–85
Universal, the, 114–115
Usury, 56–57

Visigoths, 61
Von Grunebaum, G. E., quoted, 62–63, 75, 77, 103

Wahabis, the, 72, 158–159
Walzer, Richard, 103
    quoted, 104–105
Watts, Montgomery, 18
Wealth, 43
West, the, 7, 59, 124–125, 130, 132, 154, 160, 162–165
    Muslims and, 2–3, 70
West Africa, 55, 97
Wilmette, Illinois, 85
Women's rights, 57, 82, 84, 96, 162, 164
World War I, 69, 163
Worry beads, 36

Yathrib, 7
Yemen, 6, 12, 77
Yemenis, 12, 14, 18, 23
Yom Kippur, 24–25
Yurts, 142

Zaidis, 77
Zamzam, well of, 16, 47
Zoroastrianism, 74
Zoroastrians, 12, 123